COMMON SENSE:
Your Way Through College
WORKBOOK

Information Compiled
By
Henry O. Adkins

Sixth Edition Summer 2014

ISBN 0-9672605-4-X
Copyright 2007
By Henry O. Adkins, MPA

Foreword

Every effort has been made to produce a workbook that covers the subject of the workshop that is informative and factual. Information was researched and gathered from Newspaper, periodicals and the internet. All researched sources are cited throughout the workbook.

Privacy Notice

The material contained in this Workshop workbook is solely intended for the individual and private use of the participants of the workshop. Prohibited use includes but is not limited to the copying, renting, leasing, selling, distributing, transmitting or transfer of all or any portions of the material, or use for any other commercial and/or solicitation purposes of any type without the expressed written permission from the Author and Publisher.

Contents

Your Mission Statement

It is your mission and responsibility to make sure you give yourself every opportunity to achieve all your dreams and goals in life. Getting through and graduating from College will guarantee you a better chance at becoming Successful in life.

Introduction

College Success
Is Just Common Sense

Introduction

College Success Is Just Common Sense

In the early sixties, I was a college student at Arlington State College in Arlington, Texas. I had very little, and most of the time, no money. I wore blue jeans and sandals until the first frost. After that I wore tennis shoes. I did not live on campus. I was told that I could not live in the dormitory because there was a Texas State law that prohibited colored students from living with white students at a State school. I did not believe or accept that. It sounded like *"stuff"* to me. Bull Stuff. To go to college at that school, Arlington State College, I needed to use Common Sense. It was clear to me that the administration, the staff and the faculty was going to do everything in their power to discourage me from attending that state school. I was not wanted there and it would make a lot of people happy if I left. I had to come up with an effective strategy if I was going to stay at that school and manage to live there. I found a small shot-gun house in the colored part of town. The people in the community were glad to have me there and everybody looked out for my well being. The elders of the community became my protectors. They were proud of me. They called me College Boy or they referred to me as "that College Boy." I didn't mind that at all. I made it my business to get to know the names of as many people in the community as I could, and I believed they all knew me. I didn't have a car and I never thought I needed one. I rode my bicycle to school, all around the campus and all over the town. I had a monthly meal card and I was frugal in using it. My parents bought me food at least twice a month. It was helpful that my father was the assistant manager of the grocery store in our town. There was never a chance of me starving to death. I didn't have much money, a car or the latest fashions, but I did have food, and I went to class.

Going to class was a major priority, having stuff was not. Several "Negro" students I knew at school dressed sharp everyday and some of them even carried brief cases. I wore plain simple clothes. I had an Army backpack full of books and my musical instruments. I was happy, real happy. Just acting like somebody with good sense, because I did have common sense. Some of the students I met at school felt sorry for me. They thought of me as a poor pitiful kid because I did not desire "stuff" like they did. I was asked questions like: "How do you make it? You're so poor!" I knew we didn't have much money, but we never missed a meal. My family had a car and we owned our home. I ignored anybody who tried to feel sorry for me. I felt good about myself and I did not accept their pity. I was doing what I thought I was supposed to do; and that was to go to class, study hard and pass my courses. That's what I did. Sometimes it was not easy. I had professors who would stand before the whole class and say, "if you are of the colored persuasion, you can not make more than a **D** in my class." I took those professors at their word and dropped their classes or transferred to another class on that same day. If I hadn't taken those teachers at their word when they told me what to expect from them and stayed in their class to make a point; I would not have been using common sense. Several African-Americans students ignored what they heard and stayed in those classes and received Ds and Fs, even though they did work that deserved a higher grade. They did not use common sense and ended up with bad grades on their permanent transcripts.

Many of those students saw me as a poor country boy from Terrell, Texas. They came on the Arlington State College campus daily, where they met to play cards, look good, dress sharp, and be seen driving their nice cars. After their third year they were still taking freshman English, while I completed my two year program in music and moved on to another school where I graduated with my B.S. Success for them was having stuff and wearing the latest fashions and driving the right car. What a shame and pity. What a waste of talent! Their priorities were misplaced. Success for me was going to class, passing those classes and **Graduating**. Even back then I realized that success in College was not stuff. Success was so much more. It was accomplishing something that would make me, my community and my family proud. Being Successful in College was not and never will be about "stuff."

Excerpt from Life Lessons/"Common Sense: Your Way To Success" by Henry O. Adkins

PART I

COMMON SENSE:
Plan for your College Success

A College Degree and Your Success

According to a U.S. Census Bureau report, over an adult's life, high school graduates can expect, on average, to earn $1.3 million; those with a bachelor's degree, $2.1 million; and, for people with a master's degree, $2.5 million. The Bureau of Labor Statistics (BLS) breaks down to a weekly average, with high school graduates earning approximately $656, while there college-degreed counterparts earn between $1,025 and $1,532.

The BLS also indicates that college graduates are also less affected by unemployment, with high school graduates unemployment rate at 9.7 percent compared to 5.2 percent for college graduates. The percentage of jobs requiring some college or above is expected to reach 62 percent in the near future. A college degree opens doors that would otherwise be closed to anyone with only a high school education. The number of U.S. citizens with a college degree is less than 30 percent. Receiving a college degree sets you apart and puts you in a better position for success.

Advanced Placement (AP) Credit

Advanced Placement (AP) classes can earn students high school and college credit. Students must test on the material studied and earn a score of 3 or better to receive college credit.

A clearly stated AP policy is one that allows students who perform well on AP Exams to earn credit, place out of introductory courses, or both. It also helps students move directly to material at their level and identify their academic interests. Earning credit for qualifying AP Exam scores allows students more flexibility in their college curriculum, making it possible to pursue honors programs, double majors, and study-abroad programs while still graduating on time.

Each college and university determines its own policies regarding AP Exam scores, which may include granting credit, advanced placement, or both. The AP Program defines these policies as the following:

- **Granting credit** reduces the number of credit hours required for graduation.
- **Awarding advanced placement** allows a student to place out of the introductory course that is comparable to the AP course and move directly into the next, higher-level course.

In many cases, taking an AP course fuels a student's appetite for further studies in that subject and often increases the likelihood that they will major or minor in that subject in college.

From College and University Services, Advanced Placement Program

College Level Examination Program (CLEP)

The College-Level Examination Program (CLEP) allows students to demonstrate that they have acquired college-level mastery of course content in 33 different subject areas. Students who successfully complete a CLEP exam can:

- **Enrich their degree programs** with higher-level courses in the same discipline
- **Expand their horizons** by taking a wider array of electives
- **Avoid the need to repeat material** that they already know

For students who are able to pursue their degrees only part-time, or who are struggling to meet the rising cost of higher education, CLEP offers an educationally sound, responsible way to shorten the path to a college degree. This benefit makes earning a degree more feasible—making it more likely that part-time or financially strapped students will continue working toward a degree.

College faculty design and set the standards so that any college can rely on their validity, and any student who has mastered the course material can demonstrate that mastery.

Dual Credit Courses

Students earn dual credits for classes that meet both high school and college requirements. Dual credit courses are taught in high school, at local colleges and through distance education.

All students should have the opportunity to take dual credit coursework. Talk with your high school counselor to get more information on:

- The costs involved (typically students pay reduced tuition and fees, but costs vary considerably depending upon the college offering the coursework).
- The transferability of the course credits across many colleges and universities.

The International Baccalaureate (IB) Diploma Program

The International Baccalaureate (IB) Diploma Program is a study option administered by the International Baccalaureate Organization (IBO). The IB Diploma Program is a comprehensive and balanced 11th and 12th grade curriculum and assessment system that requires students to study courses across all disciplines. Within this structured framework, the IB Diploma Program provides a great deal of flexibility, accommodating student varied interests and abilities.

The IB Diploma Program aims to develop inquiring, knowledgeable and caring young people who help to create a better and more peaceful world through intercultural understanding and respect.

What is the Diploma Programme?
http://www.ibo.org/diploma/

The IB Diploma Programme is designed as an academically challenging and balanced programme of education with final examinations that prepares students, normally aged 16 to 19, for success at university and life beyond. The programme is normally taught over two years and has gained recognition and respect from the world's leading universities.

The curriculum

IB Diploma Programme students study six courses at higher level or standard level. Students must choose one subject from each of groups 1 to 5, thus ensuring breadth of experience in languages, social studies, the experimental sciences and mathematics. The sixth subject may be an arts subject chosen from group 6, or the student may choose another subject from groups 1 to 5.

In addition the programme has three core requirements that are included to broaden the educational experience and challenge students to apply their knowledge and understanding.

The extended essay is a requirement for students to engage in independent research through an in-depth study of a question relating to one of the subjects they are studying.

Theory of knowledge is a course designed to encourage each student to reflect on the nature of knowledge by critically examining different ways of knowing (perception, emotion, language and reason) and different kinds of knowledge (scientific, artistic, mathematical and historical).

Creativity, action, service requires that students actively learn from the experience of doing real tasks beyond the classroom. Students can combine all three components or do activities related to each one of them separately.

Assessment

Students take written examinations at the end of the programme, which are marked by external IB examiners. Students also complete assessment tasks in the school, which are either initially marked by teachers and then moderated by external moderators or sent directly to external examiners.

The diploma is awarded to students who gain at least 24 points, subject to certain minimum levels of performance across the whole programme and to satisfactory participation in the creativity, action, service requirement. The highest total that a Diploma Programme student can be awarded is 45 points

Quality assurance and professional development

Any school wishing to offer the Diploma Programme and attain IB World School status must first go through the authorization process. The requirements for authorization are the same for all schools, even though the process is administered slightly differently in each IB region. The process is designed to ensure schools are well prepared to implement the programme successfully.

This is a challenging programme that demands the best from both motivated students and teachers. Schools can access an extensive package of IB professional development for teachers and administrators and commit to ongoing professional development. Schools are required to participate in an ongoing process of review and development, using standards and practices that apply to all IB World Schools.

The Advantages of
Open Enrollment Colleges and Universities

You didn't take the SAT or the ACT or you took the test and your scores were not very good. Don't worry you can still go to college. If you can't get into college through the front door, try the back door its wide open. Find an Open Enrollment/Open Admission college or university and start your college career.

Open enrollment or open admission colleges and universities are those institutions have two criteria for student admission: state residency, a high school Diploma / GED or 18 years of age and no graduation or GED. You don't have to take and pass the ACT or SAT exams to be admitted. **If you have graduated high school or earned a GED or have some high school credits but did not graduate you are still eligible to enroll in one of these colleges or universities.**

Most of these schools will require you to take a placement exam to properly place you into the appropriate classes. These are exams in English, Writing and Math. If you complete these exams with satisfactory scores you are then placed into college level courses. If you do not acquire satisfactory passing scores you are placed into **Developmental Courses**, once these courses are completed with passing scores you are placed into the college level equivalent courses.

Most students will usually pass the placement tests and are not required to take any development courses. Those that have to take developmental courses usually will have to take only one course and the rest of their courses will be all college level. You might have gotten into college through the back door, but my friend you are in college, you made it in. So, take advantage of it and do something great with it. These colleges include:

- All Community 2-year Colleges
- Most State 4-year Colleges, and
- Many Private Colleges

NOTES
_____

_____

_____

_____

_____

_____

_____

_____

_____

_____

_____

_____

_____

_____

_____

_____

_____

_____

PART II

COMMON SENSE:
STATEGIES FOR SUCCESS IN COLLEGE

Success in College Is Your Major Goal

- Know in your heart that success is part of your life. If you believe that you will graduate from College, and you will be successful. *Proverbs 23:7 states, "For as a man thinketh in his heart, so is he:..."*

- Your goal is to receive a degree. To get that degree it takes a lot of work.

- To get that degree it takes a lot of strength. *A wise man is strong; yea, a man of knowledge increaseth in strength. Proverbs 24:5.*

Find Yourself A Good Church

Adjusting to College can be a trying time, being part of a good church can make that adjustment easier.

■ Find a church where you feel comfortable enough to become an active participant.

■ A good church will help you to develop sound relationships on and off the campus.

■ A good church will come to your campus on Sunday mornings to pick you up and after services many churches will make sure you have a great Sunday meal.

■ Getting parents involved (during orientation weekend) in the search for a Good Church is essential in making the transition from home to school.

■ Get busy at the new church and Success is yours.

Make Short-term Success Goals

- Take one semester and each class at a time
  Set Short-Term Achievable Goals

- Write down your goals for each class and
  look them over daily.

- Stay Motivated. Pump yourself up.

- Keep the big picture in mind (graduation).

- Hard work is worth it. Don't slack off.

NOTES

When The Class Doesn't Fit Don't Persist

■ Immediately drop that class.

■ Don't stay in that class praying for heavenly intervention. "It ain't coming." Know when to go.

■ Get out fast, don't chance getting a bad grade. A bad grade on your transcript will last forever. Good common sense will prevent this from happening.

■ Plan your schedule and the professors for each class.

NOTES

_____

_____

_____

_____

_____

_____

_____

_____

_____

_____

_____

Find Yourself a Role Model

- When you get to College, look for someone (another student) that has your same interests and goals.

- Look for an adult that you would like to be like.

- Evaluate that person, study the person and then emulate that person.

- Be mindful that there is always someone watching you. Whether you know it or not you are a role model for somebody.

- Develop good friendships. Good friends last forever and are more valuable than gold.

28

NOTES_____

_____

_____

_____

_____

_____

_____

_____

_____

_____

_____

_____

_____

Keep Your Word

■ When you make a commitment, make sure you keep it.

■ Don't let people, your professors, or other students down. All people are important to your successful future. So, plan for your bright future by keeping your word. A Successful Man or Woman is only worth his or her word.

■ A person is judged on what he does, not on what he says, but certainly on what he does. A person that keeps his word has built for himself a strong character and bright future.

NOTES _____

_____

_____

_____

_____

_____

_____

_____

_____

_____

_____

_____

Develop Common Sense Study Habits

- Find yourself a good place to study.

- Find yourself a good study partner or study group.

- Be consistent with your study time, make good study plans and stick to those plans.

- Take good notes in class.

- Read the text and all of the assigned readings. *Not reading is a slam dunk to flunk.*

■ Without study you don't know the material and if you don't know the material you cannot pass the course. If you don't pass the courses you don't graduate.

NOTES_____

_____

_____

_____

_____

_____

_____

_____

_____

_____

Get To Know Your Professors

- Know your professors. Your professors are faced with different styles, personalities and student expectations.

- Make sure your professors get to know you.

- Ask questions in class.

- Find out where the professor's office is, make an appointment and visit him.

- Don't forget e-mail, a great way to communicate with your professor.

- Sit where you can be seen.

NOTES_____

_____

_____

_____

_____

_____

_____

_____

_____

_____

_____

_____

Get The Help You Need

Get familiar with all of the services available to students, such as;

- Financial Aid

- Academic Counselors

- Health Counselors

- Medical Services

- Computer Center

- Student Activities Center and Tutorial Services

- Library

- Career and Placement Center

NOTES_____

_____

_____

_____

_____

_____

_____

_____

_____

_____

_____

_____

_____

_____

Get Involved With Campus Organizations

■ The different student organizations on the campus are a great help in adapting to and learning about campus life.

■ These organization include;
- Christian Centers
- Ethnic Centers
- Fraternities
- Sororities
- Political Clubs
- Spirit Band
- Jazz Band
- Concert Band
- Choir, etc...

Track Your Progress

- Keep everything. Don't throw away anything, you may need it later.

- Make a chart of where you intend to be in four to five years and what you need to do to get there.

- Make a list of the courses needed for your graduation. Once you complete a course put a line through it and go to the next course. Before you realize it, graduation is upon you.

- Periodically check with your academic advisor to make sure that you are on track for graduation.

NOTES

Major stumbling blocks to Graduation
(Partying, Playing Cards and Video Games)

■ Know when, where and who to party with, choose your running dogs very carefully.

■ Card games are great, but know when to play and know when not to.

■ Video games can last all night or for several days, know when to stop, study and go to class.

■ Binge drinking does not have to be part of college life.

■ Limit the number of parties you attend, absolutely none during the week.

■ Doing dope will get you kicked out of college and into jail. Don't do it.

NOTES

Working Your Way through College

- Realize that your school work is your first priority.

- Having a job is important, but your school work is your first job.

- You will be taking 15 to 17 hours of school work a semester, a full-time job (40 hours a week) will hurt your school work. To avoid this, work only 20 to 25 hours a week on your job.

- Try to find a job on the campus or an employer that understands that you are a college student. *Note: The Starbucks Corporation is one such company.*

Starbucks offers workers 2 years of free college
By Gregory Wallace June 15, 2014

The company announced it will offer both full- and part-time employees a generous tuition reimbursement benefit that covers two full years of classes. **The benefit is through a partnership with Arizona State University's online studies program.** Employees can choose any of more than 40 undergraduate degrees, and aren't limited to only business classes. It's yet another unconventional move from the upscale coffee retailer. Starbucks bucked the trend, for example, when it continued offering **health insurance** for both full- and part-time employees as other companies dialed back offerings and blamed Obamacare.

CEO Howard Schultz, who **retook** the company's helm in2008 and turned around the slumping business, has also stood out among his peers for backing a boost in the **minimum wage**. He has also made bold statements about gun control and Washington political gridlock. He described the new education initiative in grand terms: rebuilding the American Dream for employees, known as "partners," who are left behind in an economy that requires a degree. At the same time, the cost of education can be prohibitive. "Supporting our partners' ambitions is the very best investment Starbucks can make," Schultz said in a statement.

Starbucks did not release an estimate for how much the program would cost, in part because it does not know how many employees will sign up. The benefit is equal to about $30,000 per employee, said Starbucks spokesman Jim Olson. Most of the company's 135,000 U.S. employees are eligible, he said. Those currently pursuing studies at another institution can apply to transfer their credits to Arizona State University. Employees will not be required to stay with Starbucks after earning their degree. The university will provide enrollment, financial aid and academic advisers to help students stay with the program, Starbucks said.

First Published: June 15, 2014: 9:15 PM

Avoid The Credit Card Trap

- Don't fill out the credit card applications. If you do the companies will send you one. It's a trap!!

- Student credit card debt is a serious problem. June 8 1999, the Consumer Federation of America (CFA) convened a major press conference on student credit card debt at the National Press Club in Washington, D.C. The program featured leading consumer advocates, and mothers of two college students whose credit card debts contributed to their suicides. Stay away from credit cards.

It's a trap don't get caught.

NOTES_____

_____

_____

_____

_____

_____

_____

_____

_____

_____

_____

_____

_____

Friends and The Group You Hang With Is Important To Your Future

- Develop friendships with positive people.

- Stay Away From The Campus Party Animals.

- Develop friendships with people that are taking care of business just like you.

- The group that doesn't go to class, does not graduate.

- To avoid drop out, wipe out or flunk out "Choose Your Friends wisely."

NOTES_____

_____

_____

_____

_____

_____

_____

_____

_____

_____

_____

_____

_____

_____

Research All College and University Opportunities

■ Go On Line and research;

- Historically Black Colleges and Universities

- State Colleges and Universities

- Community Colleges (2 year schools) with residential halls

- Small Colleges (2000 students or less)

- Large Universities (8000+ students)

- Faith-Based Colleges and Universities

- Ivy League Colleges and Universities

- Single Gender Colleges or Universities

- Work Colleges

NOTES

What About The Money?
Where do I find it?

- The Financial Aid Office is one of the first places you should visit as soon as you get to the campus.
- Get familiar with the people in the Financial Aid Office.
- The Financial Aid Office can help with grants, scholarships and work study. Avoid student loans. Use loans only if you have to.
- Research Scholarship and grant opportunities on the Internet.
- Do Not over look the small scholarships and grants. The small ones add up.
- Do Not over look the small four year schools of 500-1000 students or less. They usually have some money sources for those admitted.
- There are several colleges classified as Work Colleges where tuition is **FREE** to all students that are accepted. Two of them are; Berea College, Berea, Kentucky e-mail admissions@berea.edu and College of the Ozarks, Point Lookout, Missouri www.cofc.edu .

Financial Aid 101

By <u>Kim Clark</u>

- **<u>FAFSA</u>**, <u>EFC</u>, <u>Stafford</u>, <u>PLUS</u>—Huh? Colleges seem to speak a foreign language when the subject turns to money. But the basics are simple. Financial aid is simply money that helps you pay for college. There are three kinds:
- **Grants**, also called scholarships or gift aid, are the best kind of financial aid. They are free money that you don't have to pay back. Generally, grants are awarded for one of three reasons:
- **Need:** The student has qualified as financially needy, usually by filling out the Free Application for <small>Federal Student Aid</small>
- **Merit:** The student is being rewarded for good grades, athletic skill, musical talent, etc.
- **Employment benefit:** The student or the parent qualifies for tuition assistance through an employer. Many universities, for example, give employees' children a break on tuition.

- **Loans** are debts that you have to pay back and are obviously not as good grants. Some <u>loans</u>, such as federal <u>Stafford</u> and <u>Perkins loans</u> for students, are considered financial aid because taxpayers subsidize the rates so that students can borrow at a lower cost than they would get from a bank. A few charities and schools are even offering college loans at zero percent interest. The federal government calls its <u>PLUS loans</u> for parents financial aid. But many counselors note that some parents with good <u>credit</u> can borrow more cheaply from banks than from the PLUS program.

Posted April 10, 2008

> ### Student Loan Changes
> *A number of changes to federal student loans went into effect July 1, 2010 for new and current borrowers, Among them:*

- **All federal loans are now direct** from the U.S. Department of Education, rather than through federally subsidized lenders. (Private loans from banks and other lenders are still available.)

- **Income Based Repayment** (IBR) plans that was launched the summer of 2009 have been adjusted so that married couples with student loans will no longer pay higher rates than two single student borrowers. IBR is designed for those whose income is higher. Adjustments also have been made to accommodate those whose loan debt has increased since leaving school, often due to deferred payments.

- **Interest rates on new subsidized Stafford undergraduate loans** will drop from 5.6 percent to 4.5 percent. Existing Stafford loans with variable interest rates also get a small rate drop.

- **Pell grants**, which are needs-based, have gone up $200, to $5,500, potentially reducing the need to borrow.

SOURCE: Institute for College Access and Success

Financial Aid Calendar

- **January**

  Compile financial records. File federal tax return early to speed the financial aid process.

- **February**

  File a FAFSA, listing your schools of choice, which automatically receive a report. Correct any errors on the follow-up Student Aid Report (SAR).

- **March**

  Begin checking the mail for the schools' awards report and deadlines.

- **May**

  Ensure the schools have your income tax returns, verification worksheets and other documentations. Explore the possibility of private loans soon if the total cost of school minus financial aid awards is still too high.

- **June – August**

  Sign paperwork for your student loan promissory note, and contact your chosen school's financial aid office for entrance counseling.

Work-study

The federal government subsidizes some <u>campus and nonprofit jobs</u> for students. Generally, work-study jobs are awarded only to students who the college says are financially needy. The jobs typically don't pay especially well. Students may find better-paying jobs off campus. But work-study jobs have advantages. Their earnings don't reduce the student's future financial aid awards. Their schedules coincide with the schools. They are typically on campus, which reduces any commute hassle. And they are typically limited to fewer than 15 hours a week, so they jibe with studies showing that students who work between five and 15 hours a week actually get better grades than those who don't work at all or work more hours.

NOTES_____

_____

_____

_____

_____

_____

_____

_____

_____

_____

_____

_____

_____

_____

_____

_____

PART III
Free Tuition and
A Debt-Free Education

at our College!!

Work Colleges

On each **Work College** campus, there has been a historical recognition of the value of work and an institutional commitment to promote an understanding of that value among students through establishment of a work program. These work programs help students to understand work as a tool for experiential education, as a means of serving the community, and as a place for integrating academic learning, practical knowledge, and life lived in the larger community. The colleges blend courses in liberal learning and applied studies with their own particular vision of the undergraduate curriculum. Immediate benefits of participation in work college programs include reduction of student debt, increased opportunities for community service, and practical career preparation. For more information: www.workcolleges.org.

These schools (along with others) participant in the work college program:

- College of the Ozarks
- Berea College
- Knoxville College

College of the Ozarks

Debt-Free Education

College of the Ozarks is dedicated to providing a superior education to qualified students who have financial need. Lack of funds should not keep students from attending college. The College will provide a way to meet the cost of education for every student admitted.

What is the "Cost of Education"?

The cost to College of the Ozarks for providing an educational opportunity is approximately $15,900 per year for each student. Most colleges and universities attempt to pass along a portion of this cost as tuition; this is not the case at College of the Ozarks. The college guarantees to meet all of this cost for each full-time student by using earnings from its endowment, operation of its own mandatory student work program, accepting student aid grants, gifts and other sources. In effect, each full-time student's Cost of Education is met 100 percent by participating in the work program and a combination of private, institutional and federal/state student aid.

What is the student's cash amount due for the Cost of Education?

$0.00

For More information contact:

College of the Ozarks®, PO Box 17, Point Lookout, MO 65726
1-800-222-0525

Berea College

Location: Berea, Ky.

Tuition & fees: $0

Berea College, a small, largely Christian institution, only accepts students who would otherwise be unable to afford a higher education. And then, on top of free tuition, Berea gives all freshmen a Dell notebook computer.

"We attract students of high promise with limited financial resources and then provide for them the highest-quality liberal arts education that money can't buy," said Joe Bagnoli, dean of enrollment and academic services.

Berea is a great place for extremely bright students who want a school with a lot of diversity, but don't have the means to pay for college, said Bagnoli. The school's 1,600 students hail from 40 states and 60 countries, and about a third are ethnic or racial minorities. And for those who want to expand their horizons further, Berea encourages study abroad by covering up to 75% of the total costs.

Back at home, the school also waives room and board charges for students who can't afford it, about half the population.

Students must work at least 10 hours a week, but the school makes time for fun, too. Each year, the school hosts a Mountain Day celebration, where students, faculty and staff take a day off from classes to climb nearby Fort Mountain for sunrise singing and country dancing.

Knoxville College

Tuition & fees: $0

Mission and Purpose

Knoxville College is a private, church-related, four-year, coeducational, liberal arts institution. Knoxville College was founded in 1875 as part of the missionary effort of the United Presbyterian Church of North America to promote religious, moral, and educational leadership among the recently freed men and women from slavery. The College is open to students of diverse backgrounds and cultures who seek a quality liberal arts education. The College provides a challenging and stimulating educational experience for students of demonstrated academic ability and for students of potential who have been afforded little advantage within society. The College provides various public services for the improvement of the community and promotes concerned citizenship among its constituents.

Knoxville College provides its students, regardless of their backgrounds, a distinctive opportunity for educational achievement. The College maintains a program combining preparation for professional careers with a broad education in the arts and sciences.

Debt-free Policy

Knoxville College is committed to providing a quality education without the accumulation of student debts. Through participation in the Knoxville College Work Program and other College subsidies, students can graduate from Knoxville College **debt-free.**

Tuition Free Colleges and Universities

The Cooper Union

Location: New York, N.Y.

Tuition & fees: $0

With only 1,000 students and an acceptance rate around 8%, Cooper Union is tough to get into. But it's well worth the trouble, since the school offers well-respected programs in art, architecture and engineering and doesn't charge a cent to attend.

Webb Institute

COURTESY: WEBB INSTITUTE

Location: Glen Cove, N.Y.

Tuition & fees: $0

Don't come to Webb unless you're ready to study hard: Homework takes an average of five to seven hours per night. And landlubbers need not apply: Naval architecture and marine engineering are the school's only two areas of study.

"This school is for a very focused student who knows that this is exactly what they want to study," said Rob Franek, author of the Princeton Review's annual guide, *The Best 373 Colleges* (Random House/Princeton Review, $22.99). Students told Princeton Review that one of the best parts of attending Webb is how accessible the professors are. With only 90 students, the student-to-faculty ratio is 8:1.

What's more, Webb is set on a converted 26-acre estate right along Long Island Sound, so students can hang out on the school's private beach, go boating, and play sports when they get a break from work. Students also receive free passes to the YMCA.

Another plus: Not only do most students manage to graduate debt-free, the school places 100% of its student in jobs directly after graduation. And students say that most jobs in the field pay well to boot.

Nations University
(www.nationsu.org)

Tuition & fees: $0

Nations University offers **tuition-free** <u>courses</u> in religious studies to individuals around the globe through **Internet-based learning**.

Nations University students learn biblical principles from a Christian perspective, with emphasis on real-life <u>application</u>. They desire to explore Christianity, grow spiritually, understand biblical scripture and prepare for teaching and ministry.

Through Nations University, hundreds of graduates have built their faith and become spiritual leaders in their communities.

Mission

The Mission of Nations University is to build faith and train Christian leaders around the world through affordable, accessible higher education using **<u>distance learning</u>**.

Texas A&M University to Cover Tuition
Texas Students Whose Family Income is $60,000 Or Less

Posted: 5:09 PM Sep 29, 2008
Last Updated: 10:56 PM Sep 29, 2008
Reporter: TAMU Press Release

Young Texans who are eligible for admission to Texas A&M University and whose families have incomes of $60,000 or less are now guaranteed by a new program—"Aggie Assurance"—that their tuition will be covered at no cost to them.

The program, announced by Texas A&M President Elsa Murano in her formal installation address at the university's 2008 academic convocation, was made retroactive to include the current academic year. Thus, it will begin with more than 1,500 eligible students in the university's record freshman class of 8,091. Included in that total are more than 500 in the "middle-income" category.

"Texas A&M University is expanding its commitment to low- and middle-income students through this new program," Murano stated. "The program aids students by pledging to provide enough scholarships and grants to pay tuition for all eligible students. It encourages Texans to pursue higher education at a flagship research institution and is designed to reassure students from low- and middle-income families in Texas that a college education is possible, especially at Texas A&M. As part of our land-grant mission for the state, Texas A&M University is committed to providing affordable access."

Eligible students must be Texas residents entering Texas A&M as freshmen with adjusted gross family incomes of $60,000 or less. New freshmen who meet the guidelines and maintain eligibility will be part of the "Aggie Assurance" program for a maximum of four years. To continue to be eligible for "Aggie Assurance" assistance, students must maintain a grade point average of at least 2.5.

To apply for the "Aggie Assurance" program, students must submit a Free Application for Federal Student Aid (FAFSA) by March 31. Students can apply online at www.fafsa.ed.gov .

Tuition Exemption for Aides and Substitute Teachers

Texas needs more qualified teachers. That's why the State created a program that covers tuition and some fees for Education Aides who enroll in college to become certified Texas teachers. **The exemption may only be used at public colleges or universities in Texas.**

To apply for an Education Aide Exemption (EAE), you must:

- Be a Texas resident;
- Have applied for financial aid through the college to be attended, including filing the Free Application for Federal Student Aid or by qualifying on the basis of adjusted gross income. The institution will determine whether or not the AGI method will be accepted. Effective September 1, 2008, AGI limits are as follows:
  - single independent student - 31,021 or less.
  - married independent student - 62,044 or less.
  - dependent student - 62,044 or less including student and family AGI.
- Have been employed as a full-time educational aide for at least one of the past five school years, or as a substitute teacher for 180 days of the past five school years preceding the term or semester for which the student is awarded his or her initial exemption;
- Be employed in some capacity by a school district in Texas during the full term for which the student receives the award unless granted a hardship waiver as described in Section 21.1089 of this title (relating to Hardship Provision);
- Enroll in courses leading to teacher certification;
- Register for the Selective Service or are exempt from this requirement and
- Meet academic requirements established by the college or university.

Eligibility: The school district where you are employed and the financial aid office at your school determine your eligibility for this program.

FREE 4-YEAR COLLEGE EDUCATION
For Future <u>Black Male</u> TEACHERS!!!

- Do you know any Black Males who are in Senior high school who want to go to college out of state for <u>Free?</u>
- Colleges are looking for <u>future</u> black male teachers and will send them to universities/colleges for 4 years **FREE.**
- <u>Note:</u> This opportunity is for Black MALES ONLY.
- There are 10 different participating colleges and universities.
- For complete information please visit: www.callmemister.clemson.edu/index.htm

UTA Free Tuition Program

In an effort to make higher education more accessible and affordable, the University of Texas at Arlington announced a program to grant free tuition to students from households with an income of $65,000 or less.

"The Maverick Promise is a new tuition promise to families and to students with incomes of less than $65,000, for first-time undergraduate students who are eligible for a federal Pell Grant.

The $65,000 cap began with the spring semester in January 2009. The average tuition for students enrolled in 12 hours is $8,000 per year.

Students can qualify for up to $8,000 a year in free tuition, for up to five years.

The deadline to apply is April 1st.

For more financial aid and application information, call the UT Arlington Financial Aid Office at (817) 272-3561, or visit www.uta.edu/fao.

Access and Success (TEXAS) Grant Program

Program Purpose

The Texas Legislature established the TEXAS (Towards EXcellence, Access and Success) Grant to make sure that well-prepared high school graduates with financial need could go to college.

Who can apply? Students who...

For an initial award

- Are Texas residents
- Have not been convicted of a felony or crime involving a controlled substance
- Show financial need
- Have an EFC less than or equal to 4000
- Register for the Selective Service or are exempt from this requirement
- **AND**
    o Be a graduate of an accredited high school in Texas not earlier than the 1998-99 school year
    o Complete the Recommended High School Program or Distinguished Achievement Program in high school
    o Enroll in a non-profit public college or university in Texas within 16 months of graduation from a public or accredited private high school in Texas and
    o Have accumulated no more than 30 semester credit hours, excluding those earned for dual or concurrent courses or awarded for credit by examination (AP, IB or CLEP).
- **OR**
    o Have earned an associate degree from a public technical, state or community college in Texas and
    o Enroll in any public university in Texas no more than 12 months after receiving their associate's degree.

Students entering the program from high school who continue in college and who meet program academic standards can receive awards for up to 150 semester credit hours, until they receive a bachelor's degree, or for five years if enrolled in a 4-year degree plan or six years if enrolled in a 5-year degree plan, whichever comes first.

Students entering the program based on acquisition of an associate's degree who continue in college and who meet program academic standards can receive awards for up to 90 semester credit hours, until they receive a bachelor's degree, or for three years if enrolled in a 4-year degree plan or four years if enrolled in a 5-year degree plan, whichever comes first.

The academic requirements for continuing in the program are:

- At the end of the first year, the student entering the program from high school must be meeting the *school's* Satisfactory Academic Progress (SAP) requirements.
- At the end of his/her first year in the TEXAS Grant program, the person entering the program on the basis of an associate's degree must have completed at least 75 percent of the hours attempted, have an overall grade point average (GPA) of at least 2.5 on a 4.0 scale and must have completed at least 24 semester credit hours during the year.
- At the end of the second year in the program or later years, all students must complete at least 75 percent of the hours attempted in the prior academic year, have an overall college grade point average (GPA) of at least 2.5 on a 4.0 scale and complete at least 24 semester credit hours per year.

Where can awards be used?

A TEXAS Grant may be used to attend any public institution of higher education in Texas.

How much can be awarded?

The award amount (including state and institutional funds) is equal to the student's tuition and required fees. For 2008- 2009, the state amount is approximately: $2,640 per semester for public universities and state college students $865 per semester for

70

public community college students and $1,325 per semester for public technical college students.

How can you apply?

You apply for the TEXAS Grant when you complete and submit the Free Application for Federal Student Aid (FAFSA) or other application as required by your college's financial aid office. Funding is limited, so you need to submit your application as soon as possible after January 1 of your senior year. The financial aid office at each college and university will determine if TEXAS Grant is part of the aid package that is offered to you.

For More Free Tuition: www.collegefortexans.com

Free Tuition for Veterans

Six states assist veterans wishing to pursue higher education by offering a complete tuition waiver at state-sponsored colleges and universities.

The following states offer tuition waivers to qualified veterans: Connecticut, Illinois, Montana, Texas, Wisconsin and Wyoming. Each state administers its own program. Check with your State's Veterans Commission for detailed information.

Free Tuition @ Harvard University

Harvard University recently announced that undergraduate students from low-income families can attend for free...no tuition and no student loans! To find out more about Harvard offering free tuition for families making _less than $ 6 0,000_ a year visit Harvard's financial aid website at:

http://www.news.harvard.edu/gazette/daily/2006/03/30-finaid.html or call the school's financial aid office at (617) 495-1581.

Free Tuition At Georgetown College of Kentucky
The Bishop College Scholarship Program

The Overwhelmingly white Georgetown College of Kentucky is leading a $27 million campaign to preserve the memory and spirit of black Bishop College of Dallas, Texas which closed in bankruptcy nearly 20 years ago.

- By offering a Bishop College legacy Scholarship, which covers tuition.
- The first four Bishop scholarship students enrolled at
- Georgetown the 2007 fall term.

Contact the College at: www.georgetowncollege.edu for scholarship information.

Student Loan Forgiveness

Forgiveness by Teaching at a low-income School

Anyone can qualify for up to $17,500 of forgiveness by teaching at a low-income school for at least 5 years. A low-income school is designated by the United States Department of Education. Once you have completed five years of teaching in a low-income school, you may begin the federal student loan forgiveness application process.

Cancellation of Student Loans with Peace Corp Service

Peace Corp Volunteers with Perkins loans are eligible for a partial cancellation benefit. Fifteen percent of your Perkins loans can be cancelled upon the completion of each 365 days of service during your first two years of service, and 20 percent can be cancelled upon completion of each of the third and fourth years. **Therefore, four full years of service would equal a 70 percent cancellation of your existing loan**.

Segal AmeriCorps Education Award
To Re-pay Student Loan

After successfully completing a term of service, AmeriCorps members who are enrolled in the National Service Trust are eligible to receive a Segal AmeriCorps Education Award. You can use your Segal AmeriCorps Education Award to pay education costs at qualified institutions of higher education, for educational training, or to repay qualified student loans. **The award is $4,725 for a year of full-time service**, and is prorated for part-time. You can access the award in full and part, and can take up to seven years after your term of service has ended to claim the award.

73

Tuition-Reimbursement

The concept of Tuition-Reimbursement is simple enough. Corporate tuition reimbursement programs allow employees to continue learning while their company pays for their education. The organization benefits from the workers' increased professional knowledge, and employees can increase their earning power. An estimated half of today's major corporations either pre-pay or reimburse 100% tuition. Studies have shown that approximately 75% of all companies having a staff of twenty or more participate in some form of tuition reimbursement plan, and Human Resource Management reports that some major corporations are willing to pay out between $16 billion and $55 billion in education fees.

Important Point of Information. Some (not all) Tuition-Reimbursement packages require you to stay with the company for a stipulated amount of time. If you don't, you may have to pay back the full tuition. Plus, some organizations only pay for courses fitting the professional development that benefits the company. Consequently companies can restrict your paid learning to certain types of courses.

Debt "FREE" Education
DALLAS COUNTY COMMUNITY COLLEGES

THE RISING STAR SCHOLARSHIP PROGRAM

What is Rising Star Scholarship Program?

The DCCCD Foundation believes everyone should have a chance to realize the American Dream. We also believe that a college education through the Dallas County Community College District is an excellent first step toward achieving that goal. Recognizing that there are those who truly lack the personal finances needed for college - even the affordable rates offered by the DCCCD - the Foundation has established the Rising Star Scholars Program.

Rising Star provides academic support services and **up to $4,000** for tuition and books throughout your education in the DCCCD.

The scholarship initiative essentially eliminates financial need as a barrier to higher education in Dallas County. The Rising Star program promises the youth of Dallas County that if they stay in high school, graduate, demonstrate a modest level of academic potential, and have specific financial need, the Foundation will guarantee them the opportunity to earn a two-year college education from any one of the seven Dallas County Community Colleges or the El Centro College Bill J. Priest Campus

Who qualifies for Rising Star? You qualify for Rising Star if you're a graduating senior who:

- **Attends any Dallas County public high school or Dallas CAN! Academy**
- Meets eligibility guidelines for financial assistance
- Graduates in the top 40% of your class or has at least a "B" average OR passes the required skills assessment exam before enrolling in college classes.

FREE PUBLIC HIGH SCHOOL ASSOCIATE DEGREE EDUCATION PROGRAM

High school students have been earning dual credits for years, allowing them to begin college with a few hours under their belts. But at **Richland College collegiate high school** on its Abrams Road campus, students earn high school diplomas and associate's degrees simultaneously. This is the first such charter high school in the state of Texas.

OVERVIEW

The Richland Collegiate High School accepts applications for admission to the 11th grade starting on December 1 of each year. Students who live in the following counties are eligible to attend the RCHS:

- Collin County
- Dallas County
- Denton County
- Ellis County
- Kaufman County
- Rockwall County
- Tarrant County

If the Collegiate High School receives more than 200 applications for admission, federal law requires that a lottery be held to select 200 students for admission.

FOR MORE INFORMATION CONTACT:

RCHS Staff/Richland College
12800 Abrams Road
Dallas, TX 75243-2199
Office Phone: 972-761-6888

Dallas ISD's Early College/High School

By MACARENA HERNÁNDEZ/The Dallas Morning News (re-print)
mhernandez@dallasnews.com

This may be the official first day of school, but students at the Dallas school district's new **Early College High School** have been doing homework much of the summer.

The new school, which opened with 111 freshmen, is designed to encourage such thinking-ahead questions. Early college high schools allow students to work toward high school diplomas and up to 60 hours of college credit at the same time. They're usually collaborations between school districts and colleges. **The Dallas Independent School District is working with Cedar Valley College to provide the new school.**

The concept of earning college credits while in high school – usually through dual credit or Advanced Placement courses – is not new. But early college high schools often take students who would not normally enroll in such courses and provide support to help them prepare for college. The model picked up momentum in Texas a couple of years ago as a public-private alliance called the Texas High School Project and the Legislature began pushing for a college-ready culture in high schools.

Twelve new schools have opened recently, bringing the statewide total to 33, according to the Texas Education Agency. DISD already has one other early college high school with **Mountain View College** and another program with **El Centro College** that is evolving into one. The Carrollton-Farmers Branch district has one with **Brookhaven College**, and Cedar Hill ISD is opening one this school year, also with **Cedar Valley College**. DISD's new school is geared toward students whose parents didn't go to college, especially kids who may think higher education is financially out of reach. The school's staff worked particularly hard to recruit black and Latino males, groups among the least likely to earn college degrees.

Dallas Texas Skill Quest Program
Free College Tuition Program
www.skillquestntx.org

Skill Quest can help you get into a new career. The program provides assistance to qualified adults to get a professional certification and/or a two year **associate degree** at Dallas and Collin county community colleges.

1. The program pays for tuition and books.
2. It provides a Career Counselor/Navigator to help succeed in College.
3. If needed, it will assist with childcare payments.
4. After graduation, it will assist with career placement. Contact program @ 214.421.3555

Debt-Free College Education for Single Parents
Texas College Single Parent Action Network

The mission of TC-SPAN, (Texas College Single Parent Action Network) is to provide an educational opportunity for single parents and their children in an intellectual Christian atmosphere and to address the spectrum of social, emotional and economic needs of single parents and their children.

- **Academic**

  Provide the opportunity for single parents to obtain an associate's degree or a bachelor's degree within the designated years of study.

- **Economic**

  Services are provided to transport TC-SPAN students and children to scheduled destinations. TC-SPAN will provide information to identify resources to assist with cost of food, medicine, etc.

- **Child Care**

    Texas College Child Development Center provides high quality for children of the TC-SPAN program.

- **Financial Aid** *Info from www,texascollege.edu*

    The Financial Aid office will attempt to identify as many financial aid sources to assist you with the cost of your education.

- **Housing**

    Southwest Pines is an apartment community created for families like yours with beautifully landscaped grounds offering a serene and peaceful atmosphere.

AARP Foundation Women's Scholarship Program

What is the AARP Foundation Women's Scholarship Program?

The AARP Foundation's Women's Scholarship Program provides scholarship funds to women 40+ seeking new job skills, training, and educational opportunities to support themselves and their families. The AARP Foundation Women's Scholarship Program is available to eligible individuals with moderate to lower incomes and limited financial resources.

Who is eligible to apply?

To be eligible for the scholarships, applicants must be:

- Women.
- Age 40 or over by August 31.

- Able to demonstrate financial need. Enrolled in an accredited school or technical program within 6 months of the scholarship award date.

Who is this scholarship program especially trying to help?

The program does not provide assistance for graduate degree programs. It seeks women who are entering 2-3 year technical or skills up-grading programs or in the final stages of their college experience. Priority is given to women who are:

- Returning to the workforce after an extended absence.
- Underemployed (in a job with limited pay, limited growth opportunities and limited benefits).
- Raising another family member's child/children, such as grandparents raising grandchildren (with the ability to demonstrate significant financial responsibility for those child/children).
- Do I have to be a full-time student to receive a scholarship? No, you can be either a full-time or a part-time student. For More Information: http://www.aarpfoundationwlc.org/

Check this out with your College Financial Aid Office.

If you make less than $80,000/year, college grants and financial aid may be available for up to $5,645 to help you go back to school if you qualify.

Free Tuition for Senior Citizen 65 or Older

Program Purpose

To encourage senior citizens to continue their education and keep involved with local colleges and universities.

Eligibility Requirements

- Texas residents, nonresidents or foreign students;

- Enroll at a college or university whose governing board has chosen to offer this program;

- Enroll in a class that is not already filled with students who are paying full price for the courses (If the class is too small to accommodate both regular students and senior citizens, the regular students must be given priority); and

- Enroll in classes for which the college receives tax support (i.e., a course that does not depend solely on student tuition and fees to cover its costs).

- New Requirements Fall, 2014 Senate Bill 1210 (83rd Texas Legislature, Regular Session) adds a Grade Point Average requirement for persons to receive continuation awards through the program. The Bill also establishes a Limit to the Total Number of Hours, cumulative, that a student may take and continue to receive awards through this program. These changes go into effect in fall, 2014. Contact your institution for more information.

Eligible Institutions

Available only for use at a Texas public college or university. To access listings of Texas public colleges and universities, follow the links to Texas Public Institutions.

Award Amount

The maximum award is tuition for up to six hours per semester.

Note: The award does not cover fees charged for the classes. It only covers tuition. No funds may be used to pay tuition for continuing education classes for which the college receives no state tax support.

Application Process

Contact the college registrar to find out if the college or university offers this program. Then, provide proof of eligibility.

Summary Texas Tuition Exemption 65 or older

The Texas Higher Education Coordinating Board provides a tuition exemption for Texas residents who are older than 65 years of age. The exemption is available for two-year and four-year courses of study at public universities. The Texas Higher Education Coordinating Board also provides a grant for a discount on tuition at accredited public schools for up to **six semesters (18hrs)**. These grants are non-renewable, and they depend on the availability of space. Interested senior citizens may get in touch with the financial aid office, admissions or registrar's office for application information in each Texas accredited public university.

More Free College Resources

1.) Wake Forest University has an opportunity for minority students to attend its MBA program for **FREE**, and so far, the response has been very poor. Please pass along this opportunity to your friends, families. This is a great school and a tremendous opportunity to attend a top graduate school. See the details below, the contact person is:

Derrick S. Boone, Ph.D., Associate Professor of Marketing, Rm. 3139, Worrell Professional Center, Babcock Graduate School of Management @Wake Forest

email: derrick.boone@mba.wfu.edu or visit www.wfu.edu phone# toll free (866) 925-3622

2.) Black Male Teachers needed. Do you know any Black Males who are seniors in high school who want to go to college out of state for **FREE?** The CALL ME MISTER program offered by 4 historical black colleges in South Carolina,

- Benedict College
- Chaflin University
- Morris College and
- South Carolina State University

3.)   Harvard University is offering **free tuition** to families of HONOR STUDENTS and their income is less than $125,000 per year. Visitwww.fao.fas.harvard.edu or call 617.495.1581

4.)   Syracuse University School of Architecture is desperately seeking young women and men of color interested in pursuing a 5 yr. professional degree in Architecture. **Free Tuition.** Contact: Mark Robbins, Dean School of Architecture, 201 Slocum Hall, Syracuse, NY 13244-1250 (315) 443-256 www.soa.syr.edu/indes.php

5.)   APPLY NOW - If you have/know young adults between the ages of 18-31 with a High School Diploma. Can earn up to **$100,000** and earn benefits. The Federal Aviation Association is taking application for Air Traffic Controller School visit the website www.faa.gov/jobs_opportunities/airtrafficcontroller/

NOTES_____

_____

_____

_____

_____

_____

_____

_____

_____

_____

_____

PART IV

Free Education In The Form of:

GRANTS
FELLOWSHIPS
SCHOLARSHIPS
AND MORE …

Free Medical Education Military Doctors

The Navy is seeking young men and women to become Military Doctors

The Navy will totally pay for tuition, books, housing and provide a small monthly stipend.

The Navy recruits doctors from two sources:

The Health Professions Scholarship Program (HPSP) and Uniformed Services University of the Health Sciences (USUHS), the military medical school at Bethesda, Maryland.

HPSP is a scholarship program that once a student graduates, he or she commits to military service for 6 years. USUHS provides healthcare education and training to military and civilian healthcare professionals.

Either way the student graduates Medical School a **Debt-Free DOCTOR.**

For more information: www.usuhs.mil

Debt-free Nursing Scholarship

If you are between 18-28 years old, interested in the Nursing profession, the University of the District of Columbia (UDC) is offering:

- **FREE** tuition

- **FREE** books

- a $250 monthly stipend

- a guaranteed job placement as a nurse at Providence Hospital upon graduation it's a 3 year program
- annual starting salary of $40,000.

- Please contact Ms. Beshon Smith (202) 266-5481 or email Bsmith@urbanalliance.org

Columbia University
Doctor of Nursing Practice (DNP)

The new DNP program prepares nurses with the knowledge, skills and attributes necessary for fully accountable practice with patients across sites and over time. With the increasing scope of clinical scholarship in nursing and the growth of scientific knowledge in the discipline, doctoral level education is required for independent practice. Given the complexity of care, growth of information and biomedical technology, as well as an aging and increasingly diverse population with worsening disparities in care, the need for a DNP program to meet the demand for expert clinicians is timely and necessary.

NOTES

African-American Women in Computer Science
Florida A & M University

It is designed to address their absence in the field of ***computer technology***.

Dr. Jason Black is the Principal Investigator of a recently awarded $552,000 NSF (National Science Fund) Grant entitled "African-American Women in Computer Science."

The grant provides scholarships of $4000 to $10,000 per year for female, Black American students.

TALLAHASSEE, Fla. The Florida A&M University (FAMU) Computer Information Sciences (CIS) Program, housed in the College of Arts and Sciences, is the recipient of a National Science Foundation (NSF) grant valued at $552,000 dedicated to recruiting minority women to computer science and information technology disciplines. "The numbers are staggering," said Jason T. Black, Ph. D., assistant professor in CIS. "The latest data shows that out of all U.S. entering freshmen declaring a major in computer science, African-American women made up only 3.3 percent. The fact is that women are not choosing technology, and this is a dangerous predicament. When you couple that with the fact that it is estimated that 75 percent of all jobs by the year 2020 will require a technology background, it becomes a crisis call. "The program, entitled African-American Women in Computer Science, (AAWCS), is a four-year program that provides scholarships and other assistance to women who express a financial need and an interest in computer science or information technology. AAWCS, created by Black, also the principal investigator for the program, and Edward L. Jones, Ph. D., chair of the CIS program, will directly address the dismal number of minority women, particularly African-American women that pursue degrees in computer science or information technology. Women who apply to AAWCS will be accepted based on financial need, and will be awarded a scholarship of between $3,000 and $5,000 per semester. In addition to the funding, the women will participate in CIS departmental clubs and organizations, such as the Association for Computing Machinery (ACM) Club, the National Society of Black Engineers (NSBE), and the CIS Mentoring Organization (CISMO). AAWCS scholars will also be involved in other STEM programs, such as the Florida/Georgia Louis Stokes Alliance for Minority Participation (FGLSAMP) scholarship program, and the Students and Technology in Academia, Research and Service (STARS) Alliance , both NSF-funded programs. An added benefit to the students is the conference participation, where selected AAWCS scholars will be chosen to attend two national conferences, paid for by the grant, each year, such as the Grace Hopper Celebration of Women in Computing and the National Conference of Women in Information Technology (NCWIT).The AAWCS program begins operation on July 1 and will run until June 30, 2012. Applications for the program can be requested by contacting Black at jblack@cis.famu.edu or (850) 412-7354.

Undergraduate Medical Academy
Director Dennis E. Daniels, MPH, DPH

Welcome to the Undergraduate Medical Academy at **Prairie View A&M University**, a member of the Texas A&M University System. I encourage you to pay a visit to the information resources that are available to you through our web pages. It is my hope that you will find information regarding the purpose of the Academy, admissions information, medical/scientific links and much more.

Prairie View A&M University is accredited by the Southern Association of Colleges and Schools as a comprehensive public institution of higher education. The main campus is located in Waller County approximately 40 miles northwest of Houston. Prairie View A&M University, the second oldest public institution of higher education in Texas, originated in the Texas Constitution of 1876.

We have a beautiful campus, a creative and spirited student body along with a committed team of faculty and staff.

Mission

The mission of the Undergraduate Medical Academy (UMA) is consistent with the overall mission of Prairie View A&M University and the Texas A&M University System. Therefore, the Academy is dedicated to excellence in teaching, research, service, and professional development. The UMA emphasizes the integration of leadership development and pre-medical science education; without sacrificing concern and compassion for the community.

Goals

- Identify and attract top students to Prairie View A&M University by providing students with a unique study opportunity that will enhance the skills needed to enter medical school and experience a rewarding career.
- Develop a nurturing mentor cooperative network between the students of the Academy, faculty, and professionals in the medical community. Thus strengthening a successful transition for students practicing in the in the medical profession.
- Identify and develop opportunities to participate in research initiatives with faculty and participating professionals in the medical community.
- Identify students early in their educational career to foster and encourage interest in science and mathematics.

Grants

The Undergraduate Medical Academy in Partnership with Texas A&M University Health Science Center College of Medicine were awarded a grant from the Minority Health Research and Education Program in the amount of $340,000. The grant was awarded to fund the Establishment and Evaluation of Undergraduate/Medical School Partnership to Enhance Minority Student Preparation for Entrance into Professional Schools project.

Graduate Degree Fellowships and Grants

The US Department of Energy's National Energy Technology Laboratory (NETL) announces a new Academies Research Fellowship program designed to support the development of METHANE HYDRATE science and enable highly qualified postgraduate students to pursue advanced degrees in an area of increasing importance to the Nation. The 2- or 3-year fellowship will be made available to support work towards M.S. and Ph.D. degrees, or in a Postdoctoral appointment.

Graduate Study Fellowships and Foundations

Ford Foundation Diversity Fellowships for Achieving Excellence in College and University Teaching are designed to increase the diversity of the nation's college and university faculties by increasing their ethnic and racial diversity, to maximize the educational benefits of diversity, and to increase the number of professors who can and will use diversity as a resource for enriching the education of all students. Pre-doctoral fellowships support study toward a Ph.D. or Sc.D.; Dissertation fellowships offer support in the final year of writing the Ph.D. or Sc.D. thesis; Postdoctoral Fellowships offer one-year awards for Ph.D. recipients. Applicants must be U.S. citizens in research-based fields of study.

The Research Associateship Programs administer Postdoctoral (within 5 years of the doctorate) and Senior (normally 5 years or more beyond the doctorate) Research Awards sponsored by federal laboratories at over one hundred locations in the United States and overseas and are given for the purpose of conducting research in areas that are of interest to them and to the host laboratories and centers.

U.S. Department of Housing and Urban Development (HUD) Urban Scholars Postdoctoral Fellowships provide $55,000 in funding to encourage research that relates to HUD's strategic goals. Due to budget constraints at HUD, the HUD Urban Scholars Program will not be offered in 2005.

Jefferson Science Fellows spend one year at the U.S. Department of State as advisers on science policy.

Vietnam Education Foundation seeks to improve the science infrastructure in Vietnam. Fellowships are provided to Vietnamese students who wish to pursue graduate degrees in fields of science in the United States.

In the event that none of our fellowship programs are appropriate for you, we have identified other fellowship programs and lists to assist you in locating alternate funding sources for your advanced study.

If you have questions or comments, submit an email message to: infofell@nas.edu or call (202) 334-2872, or fax (202) 334-3419.

The University of Texas at Arlington
UT Arlington/Howard University Pre-Faculty Internship Program

The program (http://www.gs.howard.edu/PFF/default.htm) prepares students to enter the professoriate through a range of activities that include career planning workshops, seminars on instruction, new technologies for teaching and research, and campus visits to different institutions. At the end of the program, advanced doctoral students go through a selection process similar to an academic job search that may pair them with academic programs at partnering universities for a nine-month pre-faculty internship

The goal of the partnership is to help UT Arlington's commitment to recruit faculty of color. UT Arlington is participating in this program to help better prepare the faculty of the future and perhaps attract some of them to UT Arlington.

The agreement also could expand to other collaborative opportunities with Howard University, which produces the largest number of African American and other minority doctorate recipients from a single institution of higher education.

National Science Foundation Scholarship for Service Program

Scholarship for Service (SFS) is a unique program designed to increase and strengthen the cadre of federal information assurance professionals that protect the government's critical information infrastructure. This program provides scholarships that fully fund the typical costs that students pay for books, tuition, and room and board while attending an approved institution of higher learning. Additionally, participants receive stipends of up to $8,000 for undergraduate and $12,000 for graduate students. The scholarships are funded through grants awarded by the National Science Foundation.

Eligibility and Program Participation:

This program is ONLY open to citizens of the United States who are willing and eligible to obtain a security clearance.

- SFS Scholarship Students must serve at a Federal agency in an information assurance position for a period equivalent to the length of the scholarship or one year, whichever is longer.
- Students must have junior standing or higher and take an approved undergraduate information assurance course of study at Auburn or one of the partner universities: Tuskegee University, Alabama State University, Albany State University and

USAFA. USAFA students must be in good standing, no longer qualified for commissioned service.
- Graduate scholarships are available for students at Auburn or students from partner universities coming to Auburn for graduate work.

Scholarship Selection Criteria:
1. Motivation for a career in the U.S. Civil Service
2. Interview with Auburn Security Office (Office of Sponsored Programs)
3. Interview with scholarship committee chaired by Dr. Hamilton
4. Acceptance into the FBI's Infragard Program
5. Academic Performance*

* Undergraduate students - SAT or ACT score
- College transcript(s)
- Statement of interest for a career in the U.S. Civil Service
- Resume
- Two letters of recommendation

* Graduate students
- GRE scores
- College transcript(s)
- Statement of interest for a career in the U.S. Civil Service
- Statement of research interest in information assurance
- Resume
- Two letters of recommendation

SFS Scholarship Points of Contact:

Auburn University: Dr. Drew Hamilton
Tuskegee University: Dr. John Chen
Alabama State University: Dr. Carl Pettis
Albany State University: Dr. Stephen Owor
U.S. Air Force Academy: Dr. Martin C. Carlisle

HUD Fellowship at East Carolina University

The Master of Public Administration Program at East Carolina University has a grant from HUD to include slots for African Americans. This two-year program and all funding is provided. **There is a $9,000 stipend for the students and all tuition and fees are paid**. If selected they will be called **HUD Fellows**. Their classes will be at night because they will work as interns in a Greenville agency during the day.   Please contact:

Linda Nixon Hudson, PhD
Assistant Dean of the Graduate School
And Assistant Professor of Educational Leadership
East Carolina University
117-B Ragsdale Hall
Greenville, NC 27858-4353
(252) 328-6012/6013 main office
(252) 328-6071 (fax) Email: Hudson@mail.ecu.edu

Corporate Fellowship MA in Management
@ Wake Forest University Winston-Salem, NC
http://www.mba.wfu.edu/default.aspx?id=1133

The Master of Art in Management program is designed specifically for liberal arts majors only. The MA degree program is a 10 month intense study of the basic functional areas of business. After graduation and working for approximately two years, all MA graduates are eligible to apply to Wake Forest as part of the MA/MBA joint degree program and get the MBA in one year. The university has created a scholarship for diverse students pursuing the MA degree called the **Corporate Fellowship**..

The Corporate Fellowship provides full tuition and a $21,000 stipend to cover living expenses. Additionally, each Corporate Fellow will participate in a practicum.

The practicum has two components, educational and professional development. Each student will be assigned a mentor that is a high level executive with their sponsor corporation. The mentor will oversee an educational project covering 4 of the functional areas of business using their own corporation as the subject. The student will visit the corporation 3 - 4 times during the program to present his/her results of their research project.

Additionally, the "professional development" component of the fellowship provides career coaching and leadership development for the students. The goal for the corporation is to be able to groom and hopefully, hire a top candidate from a diverse background for their organization. Of course, there is no obligation that the students accept any offer of employment. Still, the student benefits, even if they are not ultimately hired by their sponsor corporation in that they have the MA degree and the type of experience that will make them more marketable.

The Minority Fellowship Program
http://www.samhsa.gov/minorityfellowship/

The purpose of the Minority Fellowship Program (MFP) is to reduce health disparities and improve health care outcomes of racially and ethnically diverse populations by increasing the number of culturally competent behavioral health professionals available to underserved populations in the public and private nonprofit sectors. The MFP closely aligns with the Affordable Care Act and SAMHSA's Eight Strategic Initiatives by addressing the current and projected behavioral health workforce shortages and the need to train providers on recovery-based practices. About 120 MFP Fellows are trained in an average year.

In 1973 the National Institute of Mental Health (NIMH) established the Minority Fellowship Program (MFP) to enhance services to minority communities through specialized **doctoral-level** training of mental health professionals in nursing, psychiatry, psychology, and social work. In 1992, SAMHSA was established, and the MFP was transferred from NIMH to the Center for Mental Health

Services in SAMHSA. Eligibility for this grant was expanded by Congress during fiscal year (FY) 2007 to include a fifth professional association, the American Association for Marriage and Family Therapy. In FY 2012, eligibility for this grant was expanded to also include professional counselors.

Peace Corp Fellowship Program
University of Arizona MBA/MPA degree program

- Department: Eller College of Business & Public Administration
- Degrees Awarded: Master of Business Administration (MBA), Public Administration & Policy (MPA)
- Admissions Deadlines: June 1 (Fall); October 1 (Spring). Check departmental deadlines.
- Admissions Cycle:
- Program Start: August, January for some departments.
- Founded: April 2001
- Non-resident tuition forgiveness and assistance in establishing paid internships at government and nonprofit organizations in southern Arizona and in Mexico border area. Practicum on the scholarship of engagement is available to all Fellows.

The University of Arizona is a land grant and a Research I institution, highly regarded for its graduate interdisciplinary programs. The Fellows program is available in a variety of accredited programs with a strong applied research and outreach component. The UA is developing a scholarship of engagement initiative, and has been awarded a HUD Community Development Work Study grant in Planning and Public Administration. Many internship opportunities are available in organizations that serve Hispanic and Native American communities. Departmental websites and Faculty Research Profiles at provide program details, research interests of faculty, and application information.

grad.arizona.edu/peacecorp/ Last updated September 29, 2008

PART V

Debt-Free Education

And Careers

Through Military Service

United States Military Academies

Serving in our military is a distinguished honor. Below you will find a synopsis about what each academy has to offer from their website. I encourage you to visit each academy's website for further information.

UNITED STATES NAVAL ACADEMY

The Naval Academy was founded in 1845 in what is now historic Annapolis, MD. The Naval Academy gives young men and women the up-to-date academic and professional training needed to be effective naval and marine officers in their assignments after graduation. Every day, as the undergraduate college of the naval service, the United States Naval Academy strives to accomplish its mission to develop midshipmen "morally, mentally, and physically." Moral and ethical development is a fundamental element of all aspects of the Naval Academy experience. As future officers in the Navy or Marine Corps, midshipmen will someday be responsible for the priceless lives of many men and women and multi-million dollar equipment. Every midshipman's academic program begins with a core curriculum that includes courses in engineering, science, mathematics, humanities and social science. This is designed to provide a broad-based education that will qualify the midshipmen for practically any career field in the Navy or Marine Corps. The Academy also provides professional and leadership training. We don't just teach the students about life in the Navy and Marine Corps. The professional classroom studies are backed by many hours of practical experience in leadership and naval operations, including assignments with Navy and Marine Corps units. The Naval Academy athletic program receives a priority much different than at civilian schools.

UNITED STATES MILITARY ACADEMY

Located in West Point, New York, the mission of the United States Military Academy is to educate, train, and inspire the Corps of Cadets so that each graduate is a commissioned leader of character committed to the values of Duty, Honor, Country; professional growth throughout a career as an officer in the United States Army; and a lifetime of selfless service to the nation.

Since its founding two centuries ago, the Military Academy has accomplished its mission by developing cadets in four critical areas: intellectual, physical, military, and moral-ethical. A challenging Academic Program provides a balanced education in the arts and sciences. All cadets receive a Bachelor of Science degree, which is designed specifically to meet the intellectual requirements of a commissioned officer in today's Army. The Physical Program at West Point includes both physical education classes and competitive athletics. Every cadet participates in an intercollegiate, club or intramural level sport each semester. This rigorous physical program contributes to the mental and physical fitness that is required for service as an officer in the Army. Cadets learn basic military skills, including leadership, through a demanding Military Program Cadets spend their third and fourth summers serving in active Army units around the world; attending advanced training courses such as airborne, air assault or northern warfare; or training the first and second year cadets as members of the leadership cadre. Moral-ethical development occurs throughout the formal programs as well as a host of activities and experiences available at the Military Academy. The foundation of the ethical code at West Point is found in the Academy's motto, "Duty, Honor, Country."

UNITED STATES AIR FORCE ACADEMY

Found at the foot of the Rocky Mountains in Colorado Springs, Colorado, The United States Air Force Academy's Core Values; Integrity first; Service before self; and Excellence in all we do, set the common standard for conduct across the Air Force. These values inspire the trust which provides the unbreakable bond that unifies the force. We must practice them ourselves and expect no less from those with whom we serve. Our vision; to be recognized worldwide as the premier developer of aerospace officers... leaders with impeccable character and essential knowledge... prepared and motivated to lead our Air Force and nation. Our mission is to inspire and develop outstanding young men and women to become Air Force officers with knowledge, character and discipline; motivated to lead the world's greatest aerospace-force in service to the nation.

At the U.S. Air Force Academy, we're in the business of building leaders. It's a lofty goal that can only be achieved with the right tools – and few tools are more powerful than a well-rounded education. The Academy is home to state-of-the-art facilities, 32 different academic majors and the highest standards. We strive for excellence in education every day, offering the quality curriculum that can only be found at the highest level. Through hands-on experience and the guidance of their professors, our cadets are preparing for exciting careers as Air Force officers. While the demands are rigorous, the rewards are obvious. Every cadet can succeed. And most will excel.

UNITED STATES COAST GUARD ACADEMY

The U.S. Coast Guard Academy is unique among the service academies in that we educate the leaders of a humanitarian force. The United States Coast Guard is the oldest life-saving service in the world. As a commissioned officer in the Coast Guard, you will be leading a force of men and women who are continually called on to serve their community, country and fellow citizens. Our mission goes well beyond academics. It is: To graduate young men and women with sound bodies, stout hearts and alert minds, with a liking for the sea and its lore, with that high sense of honor, loyalty and obedience which goes with trained initiative and leadership; well grounded in seamanship, the sciences and amenities, and strong in the resolve to be worthy of the traditions of commissioned officers in the United States Coast Guard in the service of their country and humanity. At our campus on the Thames River in New London, CT, the academy provides a four-year Bachelor of Science program with a full scholarship for each individual. We annually commission approximately 175 ensigns during graduation exercises in May. Following graduation, newly commissioned ensigns report for duty aboard cutters home ported nationwide.

Graduates of the academy are obligated to serve five years.

UNITED STATES MERCHANT MARINE ACADEMY

Located at Long Island's Kings Point, New York, the purpose of the U.S. Merchant Marine Academy is to ensure people are available to the nation as shipboard officers and as leaders in the transportation field who will meet the challenges of the present and the future. The nation's economic and security needs met by the U.S. merchant marine are compelling. Today, the United States imports approximately 85 percent of some 77 strategic commodities critical to America's industry and defense. Although we, as a nation, account for only six percent of the world population, we purchase nearly a third of the world's output of raw materials. Ninety-nine percent of these materials are transported by merchant vessels. There's a certain kind of young man and woman who pursues an education at the United States Merchant Marine Academy at Kings Point. They are special young people, willing to commit themselves to the demands, stresses and obligations of Academy life. Their reason? They recognize that when they graduate, they will be a step ahead of their friends at traditional colleges. Our Academy will teach you how to succeed in the maritime and transportation industries or the Armed Forces, while it prepares you to receive a Bachelor of Science degree, a merchant marine license, and an appointment as a commissioned officer on reserve or active duty in the U.S. Armed Forces. But most importantly, Kings Point, through its unique combination of academic, regimental and shipboard programs, will train you as a leader of quality, integrity and high ethical standards. The academic and professional credentials that you earn, and the leadership ability you acquire, will set you apart and above as you enter the career marketplace.

Reserve Officer Training Corps (ROTC) Scholarships

Scholarships are not necessary for participation in ROTC, but hundreds of ROTC students receive scholarships every year. Scholarships are competitively awarded on merit. The main considerations are:

- High school academic record
- SAT or ACT scores
- Extracurricular activities
- Personal interview

The length, value, and terms of ROTC scholarships vary by service. **All services offer four-year scholarships that include full tuition, books, fees, and a monthly tax-free stipend.** However, three, two, and even one-year ROTC scholarships are available, which are all well worth inquiring about. Some services offer health-related or Nurse ROTC program variations, and the U.S. Navy even has an ROTC program at a variety of Historically Black Colleges and Universities.

ROTC (Reserve Officer Training Corps) and Naval ROTC Programs offered by the Army, Marine Corps, Navy, and the Air Force, train qualified young men and women to become officers in those services upon graduation from college. The good news is, ROTC is available in more than 1,000 colleges and universities throughout the U.S., both those that host ROTC units or detachments and those with cross-enrollment agreements with them.

During college, students take a full course load. However, included in the curriculum are military science courses that provide the specialized knowledge needed as an officer. In addition to academic courses, ROTC candidates wear uniforms once a week during military labs, drills, military science presentations, and other practical training activities. ROTC summer programs offer a taste of military life, such as midshipmen cruises in Naval ROTC and round out a candidate's military training.

Debt-Free Law Degree Through The Air Force ROTC Program

One-Year College Program (OYCP)

General Information

The One-Year College Program (OYCP) is a one-year Air Force ROTC program for law students. OYCP students are guaranteed a position as an Air Force judge advocate upon successful completion of the AFROTC program,

1. graduation from an ABA-approved law school,
2. completion of legal licensing requirements including admission to practice law in the highest court of any state,
3. a territory of the United States, or a federal court,
4. and medical qualification.

Eligibility

Law students in their second year of law school are eligible to apply. Applicants must (1) be attending an ABA-approved law school which has, or is located near, an AFROTC detachment, (2) be in good academic standing, and (3) meet AFROTC entry standards, such as U.S. citizenship, Air Force Officer Qualification Test minimum scores, and AFROTC weight and medical standards. The selectees for this program must be under age 35 at the time of commissioning.

As part of this program, applicants must contact their local AFROTC Detachment (where the applicant plans to receive training) during their second year of law school. The applicant should ensure the detachment is willing to enroll them as a cadet if The Judge Advocate General selects them for the OYCP and if otherwise eligible. In their application, applicants should include a letter from the ROTC detachment indicating that the applicant has met with the detachment personnel in preparation for applying to the JAG board. A list of ROTC detachments can be found at http://www.afrotc.com/colleges/detLocator.php. Upon completion of the application, applicants schedule a hiring interview with the senior attorney (staff judge advocate - SJA) at <u>any active duty Air Force base</u>. The deadline for completion of the application paperwork and the hiring interview is February the first of each year.

Selection is on a best-qualified basis. Selection factors include academic performance, extracurricular activities, community service, prior military record (if any), work experience, and the SJA recommendation. The Judge Advocate General selects the best-qualified applicants based upon the recommendations of a board of senior judge advocates. The selection board convenes in February each year. Applicants are notified of the results by letter.

Training

Selectees attend an AFROTC field training encampment at an Air Force base during the summer before their third year of law school. They complete the normal academic requirements for the AFROTC program while attending their third year of law school.

Commissioning and Service Commitment

Upon completion of the AFROTC program and graduation from law school, OYCP cadets are commissioned as second lieutenants in an inactive status. Those who have completed legal licensing requirements normally enter active duty shortly thereafter. Those who have not yet completed legal licensing requirements are granted an educational delay until completion of those requirements. The initial active duty commitment is four years. Graduates of the OYCP begin active duty as first lieutenants and are eligible for promotion to captain on the day they complete six months of active duty.

Financial Assistance

OYCP/AFROTC students are eligible for a **tax-free** stipend each month. Students should also consult the ROTC website for other eligibility requirements.

NOTES_____

_____

_____

_____

_____

_____

_____

_____

_____

_____

ROTC Chaplain Internship Program (CHIP)
ROTC Education Delay Program for Chaplaincy Studies

The ROTC Education Delay Program offers ROTC Cadets the opportunity to apply for a delay in the fulfillment of their Active Duty Service Obligation (ADSO) in order to become an Army Chaplain.

1. Cadets normally apply for an education delay at the same time and on the same form (FORM 67-9) that they use to submit their choice of a branch selection, usually between the months of May and September before their senior year of college. The Army approves education delays on a case-by-case basis through a board process.

2. Once a cadet is granted an Education Delay by USA Cadet Command (USACC), the cadet then contacts an Army Chaplain Recruiting Team (CRT) in order to submit an application packet for a Chaplain Candidate Accessions Board. Should the cadet not be accessed by this board, or should the cadet neglect to submit an application for accessing, the cadet would then be branched by USACC in accordance to their original obligation.

3. Once a cadet is accessed as a Chaplain Candidate, they are entitled to all the benefits of and responsibilities of the CCP except Tuition Assistance. Cadets can contact their PMS, the USACC chaplain, or a CRT.

ROTC Chaplain Internship Program (CHIP)

The United States Army Cadet Command (USACC) offers summer internships at selective Army posts for selected cadets during their junior year in order to explore the chaplaincy. For more information cadets should contact their PMS or USACC chaplain.

http://www.usachcs.army.mil/

Military Chaplaincy Program

Established by the Second Continental Congress in 1775, the Army Chaplaincy predates the Declaration of Independence and is both the largest and oldest military chaplaincy in the world. More than 25,000 chaplains have served since then in 36 wars and 242 major combat engagements. Six were awarded the nation's highest military award for valor (The Medal of Honor). Many former Army Chaplains have served in prominent positions of government, education and religion. Today, as in the past, chaplains serve in a great variety of positions and places throughout the world. While their methods of ministry may change with the transformation of the battlefield, their ministry and message are timeless and immeasurable.

No matter what your faith group, the Army Chaplaincy offers various ways for you to serve both God and your Country. From providing support to Unit Ministry Teams as a Chaplain Assistant, to caring for the spiritual well-being of Solders and their families as an Army Chaplain, you'll discover the opportunities are as varied as they are unique.

As a **Chaplain Officer**, you will lead a Unit Ministry Team (UMT), which consists of you and a trained Chaplain Assistant. As an Army Chaplain you will have the responsibility of caring for the spiritual well-being of Soldiers and their families. Army Chaplains are the spiritual leaders of the Army and they perform religious ceremonies from births and baptisms, to confirmations and marriage, to illness and last rites.

Join While Still Studying For The Ministry. You do not need to wait until ordination to join the Army Chaplaincy. You can train to become an Army Chaplain at the same time you are training for the ministry. The training and experience you will receive as a Chaplain Candidate will be a rich adjunct to your ministerial education and training. All Chaplain Candidates are commissioned officers assigned to the Army Reserve in the Staff Specialists Branch.

Should you decide to become an Army Chaplain, by participating in the Chaplain Candidate Program (CCP), you will have a head start on entering the Army as a Chaplain, as well as enjoying the many benefits and privileges associated with being an Army officer.

Chaplain Basic Officer Leadership Course

All Chaplain Candidates are encouraged to attend Chaplain Basic Officers Leadership Course (CBOLC). CBOLC is 12 weeks long and is offered twice a year (winter and summer). Normally a candidate does the first half of CBOLC (Chaplain Initial Military Training/CIMT and Phase 1) as soon as possible since it is a prerequisite for all other training in the CCP. It is not until the summer before their senior year that Chaplain Candidates can complete Phases II and III. Candidates who enter the CCP as seniors in school may complete all of CBOLC at once if they plan on accessioning as a chaplain following graduation.

Paid Practicums

A Chaplain Candidate is authorized up to 45 days a year to train under the supervision of a senior chaplain at a military installation. This training, called a "practicum," is offered to all candidates once they have completed the first part of CBOLC.

Practicums vary in type, to include Army Reserve Commands, Chaplaincy Recruiting, Garrison Ministries, Combat Ministries, Medical Training and Administrative Support. Some Candidates take advantage of the opportunity to earn their Parachutist Badge at Fort Benning and/or their Air Assault Badge at Fort Campbell. The most comprehensive training is one quarter of Clinical Pastoral Education (CPE) through the Medical Command involving 75 days.

Practicums, which may vary in length from a minimum of 12 days to a maximum of 45 days (except for Clinical Pastoral Education which is 75), may be done at most any time of the year.

Chaplain Candidate Requirements

To be eligible for this program, you must:

- Obtain an ecclesiastical approval from your denomination or faith group.
- Educationally, you must:
- Possess a baccalaureate degree of not less than 120 semester hours (College seniors can apply before completion of their undergraduate program).
- Be a full-time graduate student at an accredited seminary or theological school.
- Be a U.S. citizen or permanent resident.
- Be able to receive a favorable National Agency Security Clearance.
- Pass a physical exam at one of our Military Entrance Processing Stations (MEPS).
- **Must be at least 18 years of age and not older than 39 years of age at time of commissioning.**

While attending seminary, Chaplain Candidates may apply for tuition assistance through the U.S. Army Reserve. You may be eligible for up to 100% of the tuition costs, up to $250 per credit hour with a maximum cap of $4500 per year. This program requires service of at least four years in a U.S. Army Reserve unit once you become a qualified Chaplain.

Veterans Educational Assistance Program (VEAP)

VEAP is an educational assistance program that is available if you elect to make contributions from your military pay to participate in this education benefit program. The following is a summary of the VEAP.

Benefit Description

VEAP is available if you elect to make contributions from your military pay to participate in this education benefit program. The government matches your contributions on a $2 for $1 basis. You may use these benefits for degree, certificate, correspondence, apprenticeship/on-the-job training programs, and vocational flight training programs. In certain circumstances, remedial, deficiency, and refresher training may also be available.

Benefit entitlement is one to 36 months depending on the number of monthly contributions. You have 10 years from your release from active duty to use VEAP benefits. If there is entitlement not used after the 10-year period, your portion remaining in the fund will be automatically refunded.

Eligibility

To qualify, you must meet the following requirements:

- Entered service for the first time between January 1, 1977 and June 30, 1985
- Opened a contribution account before April 1, 1987
- Voluntarily contributed from $25 to $2,700
- Completed your first period of service
- Were discharged or released from service under conditions other than dishonorable.

If you are currently on active duty and wish to receive VEAP benefits, you must have at least three months of contributions available.

Contributions may be withdrawn if you do not meet the basic eligibility requirements or if you formally request a refund of the contributions withheld.

How to Apply

You should make sure that your selected program is approved for VA training. If you are not clear on this point, VA will inform you and the school or company about the requirements.

Obtain and complete VA Form 22-1990, Application for Education Benefits. Send it to the VA regional office with jurisdiction over the state where you will train. If you are not on active duty, send copy 4 (Member Copy) of your DD Form 214, Certificate of Release or Discharge From Active Duty. If you are on active duty, you must have your enrollment approved by your base Education Services Officer, and you must have your service verified by your Commanding Officer.

If you have started training, take your application and Member Copy of DD Form 214 to your school or employer. Ask them to complete VA Form 22-1999, Enrollment Certification, and send all the forms to VA.

If you wish to withdraw your contributions from VEAP, obtain and complete VA Form 24-5281, Application for Refund of Educational Contributions, and send it to your nearest VA regional office.

Visit **www.GIBILL.VA.GOV** for up-to-date information on this and other education benefits.

The Montgomery GI Bill
Educational Benefits For Selected Reserve Military
(U.S. Code, Title 10, Chapter 1606)

This educational benefit is for current members of the Army Reserve, Navy Reserve, Air Force Reserve, Marine Corps Reserve, Coast Guard Reserve, Army National Guard and Air National Guard who signed a six-year obligation to serve after June 30, 1985, or, if an officer, six years in addition to the original obligation.

What other eligibility requirements are there?

In addition to current membership in the Selected Reserve or National Guard, an individual must also have completed initial Active Duty for Training, have a high-school diploma or equivalency certificate before applying for the GI Bill benefit and remain in good standing with his or her Selected Reserve or Guard unit.

What does the program provide?

Up to 36 months of education benefits are payable 14 years from the date of eligibility or until the individual leaves the Selected Reserve or Guard.

What kinds of education qualify?

The benefit may be used for college degree or certification programs, technical or vocational training, flight training, apprenticeship or on-the-job training, and correspondence courses. Non-credit, remedial and refresher courses may be approved under certain circumstances.

Visit **www.GIBILL.VA.GOV** for up-to-date information on this and other education benefits.

The Post - 9/11 GI Bill

The Post - 9/11 GI Bill is a new education benefit program for individuals who served on active duty on or after September 11, 2001.

When Can I Receive Benefits under the Post-9/11 GI Bill?

Post-9/11 GI Bill benefits are payable for training pursued <u>on or after August 1, 2009</u>. No payments can be made under this program for training pursued before that date.

Am I Eligible?

You may be eligible if you served at least 90 aggregate days on active duty after September 10, 2001, and you are still on active duty or were honorably-discharged from the active duty; or -released from active duty and placed on the retired list or temporary disability retired list; or -released from active duty and transferred to the Fleet Reserve or Fleet Marine Corps Reserve; or -released from the active duty for further service in a reserve component of the Armed Forces.

You may also be eligible if you were honorably discharged from active duty for a service-connected disability and you served 30 continuous days after September 10, 2001.

If I am eligible for the Montgomery GI Bill, Montgomery GI Bill-Selected Reserve, or the Reserve Educational Assistance Program, am I eligible for Post-9/11 GI Bill?

If, on August 1, 2009, you are eligible for one of these programs **and** you qualify for the Post-9/11 GI Bill, you may make an irrevocable election to receive benefits under the Post-9/11 GI Bill.

Note: Once you elect to receive benefits under the Post-9/11 GI Bill, you will no longer be eligible to receive benefits under the program from which you elected the Post-9/11 GI Bill.

How much will I receive?

Based on your length of active duty service, you are entitled to a percentage of the following:

- Cost of tuition and fees, not to exceed the most expensive in-state undergraduate tuition at a public institution of higher education (paid to school);
- Monthly housing allowance* equal to the basic allowance for housing payable to a military E-5 with dependents, in the same zip code as your school (paid to you);
- Yearly books and supplies stipend of up to $1000 per year (paid to you); and -A one-time payment of $500 paid to certain individuals relocating from highly rural areas.

***NOTE** – The housing allowance and books and supplies stipend are not payable to individuals on active duty. The housing allowance is not payable to those pursuing training at half time or less or to individuals enrolled in distance learning.*

How many months of assistance can I receive?

Generally, you may receive up to 36 months of entitlement under the Post-9/11 GI Bill.

How long am I eligible?

You will be eligible for benefits for 15 years from your last period of active duty of at least 90 consecutive days. If you were released for a service-connected disability after at least 30 days of continuous service, you will also be eligible for benefits for 15 years.

Visit **www.GIBILL.VA.GOV** for up-to-date information on this and other education benefits.

Reserve Educational Assistance Program (REAP)
(Chapter 1607 GI Bill)

What Is REAP?

REAP (Chapter 1607 of title 10, U.S. Code) is a GI Bill program that provides up to 36 months of education benefits to members of the Selected Reserve, who are called to active service in response to a war or national emergency, as declared by the President or Congress.

Who Is Eligible?

A member of a Reserve component who serves on active duty on or after September 11, 2001 under title 10, U.S. Code, for at least 90 consecutive days or more under a contingency operation.

How Much Does the Benefit Pay?

The educational assistance payable under REAP is a percentage of the Montgomery GI Bill-Active Duty (MGIB) rate based on the number of continuous days served on active duty. Persons released before 90 days due to an injury, illness, or disease incurred or aggravated in the line of duty receive the 40% rate.

- Members who serve 90 days but less than 1 year will receive 40% of the MGIB 3 year rate.
- Members who serve 1 year but less than 2 years will receive 60% of the MGIB 3 year rate.
- Members who serve 2 or more continuous years will receive 80% of the MGIB 3 year rate.

The amount VA pays is based on the type of training program and training time (i.e. full time, half time, etc). If attendance is less than a month or less than full-time, payments are reduced proportionately.

Visit **www.GIBILL.VA.GOV** for up-to-date information on this and other education benefits.

Survivors and Dependents' Educational Assistance
(U.S. Code, Title 38, Chapter 35)

The Survivors' and Dependents' Educational Assistance Program provides education and training opportunities to dependents of veterans who are permanently and totally disabled or deceased because of a service-related condition, or who died while on active duty. The program offers up to 45 months of education benefits, which can be used for degree and certificate programs, apprenticeship and on-the-job training. Spouses may take correspondence courses.

This education benefit is provided to the children or spouses of military personnel and / or veterans who:

- Died in the lime of duty while on active duty
- Became totally and permanently disabled due to a service-connected cause
- Died while considered totally and permanently service-connected disabled
- Were missing in action or captured while in conflict with a hostile force
- Were forcibly detained or interned by a foreign government in the line of duty
- Are receiving hospital or ongoing outpatient treatment for a permanent and total service-connected disability while still on active duty and likely to be discharged due to that disability

The window to use it:

- The entitlement is good for 45 months of full-time payments
- For spouses, the benefit must be used within 10 years of the date of eligibility
- For surviving spouses, the benefit must be used within 20 years of the date of eligibility
- For children, the benefit must be used within eight years of the date of eligibility
- Eligibility for children to use the benefit must be established between the ages of 18 and 26.

Vocational Rehabilitation Employment VetSuccess
(Voc-Rehab Chapter 31)

The Department of Veterans Affairs' Vocational Rehabilitation and Employment (VR&E) VetSuccess program (also known as Voc-Rehab or Chapter 31) offers disabled vets counseling, training, education and other services needed to prepare for, find, and keep suitable jobs.

If you are a veteran who has a <u>VA disability</u> rating and an <u>employment handicap</u>, you may be entitled to vocational rehabilitation & employment services under Chapter 31 of the GI Bill. These services include - but are not limited to - counseling, training, education and job placement assistance.

The following services may be provided through the VR&E program:

- Comprehensive rehabilitation evaluation to determine abilities, skills, interests, and needs.
- Vocational counseling and rehabilitation planning.
- Employment services such as job-seeking skills, resume development, and other work readiness assistance.
- Assistance finding and keeping a job, including the use of special employer incentives.
- On the Job Training (OJT), apprenticeships, and non-paid work experiences.
- Financial assistance for post-secondary training at a college, vocational, technical or business school.
- Supportive rehabilitation services including case management, counseling, and referral.
- Independent living services for for Veterans unable to work due to the severity of their disabilities.

VR&E Eligibility

Eligibility and entitlement for VR&E are two different things. You may meet eligiblity criteria, yet not be entitled to services. The first step in the VR&E process is to be evaluated to determine if you qualify for services. To receive an evaluation for VR&E services, you must meet the following "eligibility" criteria:

- Have received, or will receive, a discharge that is other than dishonorable.
- Have a service-connected disability rating of at least 10% - or a memorandum rating of 20% or more from the VA.
- Submit a completed application for VR&E services (online at the Department of Veterans Affairs VONAPP site).

Period of Eligibility - Like many VA benefits VR&E has a limited period of eligibility. The basic period of eligibility in which VR&E services may be used is 12 years from the date of separation from active military service, or the date the veteran was first notified by VA of a service-connected disability rating, which comes later.

The basic period of eligibility may be extended if a Vocational Rehabilitation Counselor determines that a veteran has a Serious Employment Handicap.

Visit **www.GIBILL.VA.GOV** for up-to-date information on this and other education benefits.

Career Opportunities in U.S. Army Bands

Make Your Passion Your Profession

Dating back over 230 years to the Revolutionary War, musicians have served a vital role in the Army by upholding tradition, entertaining our Soldiers, and serving as musical ambassadors of our nation. Today, the US Army is the oldest and largest employer of musicians in the world. With assignments around the world and a long list of benefits, the Army Bands Program offers talented musicians a unique opportunity to do what they do best — play music. If you're interested in earning a living while embracing your passion for music, then check out what the Army Bands Program has to offer you.

Whether you are a professional musician looking for a full-time gig or a college student interested in part-time employment, Army bands are a great opportunity for any serious musician.

Active Duty-Traditional Army Bands (MOS 42R)

Members of Army Bands are involved in the vibrant tradition of performing at Army ceremonies, parades, concerts, festivals, dances and many other events. Musicians perform in a variety of ensembles ranging from ceremonial band to jazz band to small ensembles, playing all styles of music. If you are looking for full-time employment as a musician, the Army may be the perfect fit. With over 30 locations across the U.S. and overseas, the active duty Army bands offer musicians the ability to perform music for a living while earning great benefits from the military.

Active Duty-Special Army Bands (MOS 42S)

The four special Army bands have a long standing tradition of excellence and perform at the most prestigious events in the US and overseas including presidential inaugurations, foreign dignitary visits, funeral services at Arlington Memorial Cemetery, along with regularly scheduled public concerts and tours. For information on these bands and their vacancies, please click on the links below.

- THE OLD GUARD FIFE & DRUM CORPS
- THE UNITED STATES ARMY BAND "PERSHING'S OWN"
- THE UNITED STATES ARMY FIELD BAND
- U.S. MILITARY ACADEMY BAND

Army Reserve and National Guard Bands (MOS 42R)

The Army's 18 Reserve and 53 National Guard Bands meet one weekend a month and two weeks a year to rehearse and perform for their local communities as representatives of the US Army. Army Reserve and National Guard Bands offer opportunities to serve part time while pursuing higher education or continuing your career in the civilian sector. This is a popular choice for college students and professional musicians alike.

Army Band Officer-Conductor (MOS 42C and MOS 420C)

Music offers exciting careers in the Army with significant opportunities for advancement. Every year, the Army Band program selects one or two highly qualified individuals via competitive auditions to serve as Army Bands Officers. These Officers rotate through a variety of positions: associate conductor (executive officer), administrator and instructor at the Army School of Music. After several years of experience, they may also serve as commander and principle conductor of an Army band.

Learn more about career opportunities as an officer in the Army Bands Program

Musicians with an interest and experience in conducting can also consider becoming a **band officer** through the Warrant Officer program. Warrant Officers are selected from the enlisted musicians in the band to be the commander and conductor of the band. Selections are based on strict criteria along with a series of auditions. The first step towards your career as a Warrant Officer in the Army Bands is to enlist as a musician.

http://www.bands.army.mil/careers/

NOTES_____

_____

_____

_____

_____

_____

_____

_____

PART VI
A List of Scholarships

Scholarships Are Out There

There are many scholarships available but most students are not aware of their existence. There are scholarships available for the most popularly known sports, such as:

- Academics
- Football
- Basketball
- Track
- Baseball

There are other somewhat known activities where scholarships are available, such as:

- Soccer
- Softball
- Tennis
- Marching Band

There are those least known activities where scholarships are available, such as:

- Wrestling
- Cheerleading
- Music
- Theater
- Swimming
- Gymnastics

Scholarships at Two-Years Colleges

Two-Year Colleges offer scholarships in all varsity athletic programs. Scholarships are awarded based on athletic ability and potential, need, and availability. You must be an accepted applicant before you can be awarded a scholarship. Two-Year Colleges have a long tradition of successful teams and individual athletes. Many of the athletes have gone on to participate and contribute nationwide in Division I, Division II and Division III programs. Athletes at many of these Colleges participate on a competitive NJCAA Division II level or higher. Most Two-Year College athletes (80% or better) graduate with an AA or AS degree then continue their athletic careers either at a four-year school or professionally.

Apply to lesser known schools and ask for a scholarship. Major schools are swamped with applicants, lesser known schools are looking for good candidates but do not have the budget to do major recruiting. Scholarships are awarded on a number of criteria, including financial need, academic or athletic achievement, nationality, ethnicity and public service. It's typically free to apply, so it can't hurt to apply for anything and everything. This a great opportunity for you, so send a letter to the school and highlight the following;

1. Grade-Point average
2. SAT/ACT scores
3. Extra-curricular activities
4. Community Service
5. If in Sports, show your Stats
6. DVD of yourself in your sport
7. News clippings, if available.
8. Letters of recommendation
9. Highlight your skills...ie...math tutor, etc...
10. Transcripts
11. Parent's Financial Information

12. Financial Aid forms
13. Proof of eligibility
14. One or more essays
15. Make yourself as attractive as possible.

A Short List of Scholarships

The Urban Scholarship Fund

The Urban Scholarship Fund (USF) is a scholarship program administered by TADC, established by the Texas State Legislature in cooperation with SBC, Verizon and Sprint. USF is for graduating high school seniors and returning students attending any nonprofit public and/or private two- or four-year college or university or technical school. Applicants must meet eligibility requirements listed on the Urban Scholarship Fund Application. Please look them up at: www.txadc.org.

100 Scholarships at Central State University

Central State University in Wilberforce, Ohio has 100 full scholarships available for the fall. This is a historically Black college and the scholarships are first come, first served.

If interested contact:

Carla Pierce, Office Manager
Maryland Mentoring Partnership
517 North Charles Street, Suite 200
Baltimore, Maryland 21201
410.685.8316 x222

The Roger and Jody Lawler Scholarship
@ Collin College (Texas)

This scholarship supports students majoring in science, biotechnology and studies relating to the environment or agriculture with **scholarships to cover tuition fees and books as well as laptop computers or other technology necessary for their coursework.** For more information about scholarships and gifts to support students, contact the Collin College foundation at 972.599.3144 or visitwww.collin.edu/foundation.

Once you have earned an Associate degree and are now ready to transfer to a four-year school, try the **Jack Cooke foundation Undergraduate Transfer Scholarship fund**. It is the largest private transfer scholarship for community college students in the nation.

Baptist General Convention of Texas
333 N. Washington Street
Suite 371
Dallas, Texas 75246-1798

Havens Foundation, Inc.
25132 Oakhurst, Suite 210
Spring, Texas 77386

Hattie M. Strong Foundation
1620 Eye Street NW, Room 700
Washington, D.C. 20006

Horatio Alger Association
99 Canal Center Plaza
Alexandria, VA 22314

James A. & Juliet L. Davis
Foundation
P.O. Box 2027
Hutchinson, KS 67504-2027

John Gyles Education Fund
P.O. Box 4808
712 Riverside Drive
Fredericton, New Brunswick
E3B 5GA Canada   *

Natl. Assn. of Negro Business
Professional Women Club
1806 New Hampshire Ave. NW
Washington D.C. 20009-3208

National Merit Scholarship Corp.
1560 Sherman Ave., Suite 200
Evanston, Ill. 60201

Negro Educational Emergency Drive
643 Liberty Ave., 17th Floor
Pittsburgh, PA 15222

Tall Clubs International
P.O. Box 1964
Bloomfield, NJ 07003-1964

Jackie Robinson Foundatioin
3 West 35th Street
New York, NY 10001-2204

Blues Haven Foundation
2120 S. Michigan Ave.
Chicago,IL 60616

Donna Reed Foundation
1305 Broadway
Denison, IA 51442

McGraw foundation
3436 North Kennicott Drive
Arlington Heights, IL 60004-1460

Merrill Lynch Foundation
World Financial Center, So. Tower
New York, NY 10080-6106

Metropolitan Life Foundation
Onee Madisn Avenue
New York, NY 10010-3690

Mars Foundation
6885 Elm Street
McLean, VA 22101-3883

Lilly Endowment
2801 North Meridian Street
P.O. Box 88068
Indianapolis, IN 46208

Kraft General Foods
Three Lakes Drive
Northfield, Il 60093-2753

Kettering Family Foundation
2833 So. Colorado Blvd.
Suite 2415
Denver, CO 80222

Joyce Foundation
Educational Foundation
135 So. LaSalle St. #4010
Chicago, IL 60603-4886

Westinghouse Foundation
11 Stanwix Street
Pittsburgh, PA 15222-1384

Apple Education Grants
One Infinite Loop, MS:38J
Cupertino, CA 95014

Angel Network Foundation
c/o Oprah Winfrey show
P.O.Box 617940
Chicago, Il. 60661

Meadows Foundation
3003 Swiss Avenue
Dallas, Texas 75204-6049

Spencer Foundation
900 North Michigan Avenue
Suite 2800
Chicago, IL 60611-1542
TRW Foundation
1900 Richmond Road
Cleveland, OH 44124

McDonald's Charities
Kroc Drive
Oak Brook, IL 60521

Leonard M. Perryman
Communications Scholarship
475 Riverside Drive, Suite 1370
New York, NY 10027

Herbert Lehman Educational Fund
99 Hudson Street, Suite 1600
New York, NY 10013

Ron Brown Scholar Program
1160 Pepsi Place, Suite 306-B
Charlotteville, VA 22901

Project Excellence
3251-C Sutton Place, NW
Washington, DC 20016

David Letterman
Telecommunications Scholarship
NBC Ed Sullivan Theater
New York, NY 10010

Oprah Winfrey
Endowed Scholarship Fund
P.O. Box 909715
Chicago, Ill 60690

American Academy of Allergy
Asthma & Immunology Scholarship
611 East Wells Street
Milwaukee, WI 53202-3889

Am. Gen. Character Stars Program
P.O. Box 23737
Nashville, TN 37203-3737

John Gyles Education Awards
P.O.Box 4808, 72 Riverside Drive
Fredericton, New Brunswick
Canada, E3B -5G4

Cable & Telecommunications Assoc.
Texas Scholarship Program
P.O. Box 1234
Dallas, Texas 75248

Stephen Phillips Scholarship
P.O. Box 870
Salem MA 01970

Horace Mann Scholarship
P.O. Box 20490
Springfield, IL 62708

Herbert Lehman Education Fund
99 Hudson Street
New York, NY 10013

USA Group Scholarship
30 South Meridian
Indianapolis, IN 46204-3503

ASMN Institute
1333 New Hampshire Ave. NW #1070
Washington, D.C. 20036

NOTES

PART VII

College Tuition Websites
and
Historically Black Colleges and Universities

Christian College Annual Tuition

Source: CCCU Tuition Survey: 2004-2005

Westmont College	$26,240.
Gordon College	$21,440.
Biola College	$20,932.
Azusa Pacific University	$20,466.
Wheaton College	$20,000.
Bethel University	$19,900.
Taylor University	$19,674.
Covenant College	$19,340.
Anderson University	$17,990.
Calvin College	$17,845.
Palm Beach Atlantic University	$16,360.
Colorado Christian University	$16,060.
Indiana Wesleyan University	$15,204.
Carson-Newman College	$14,420.
Oklahoma Baptist University	$13,162.

Oklahoma Christian University	$13,160.
Oklahoma Wesleyan University	$13,100.
Southwest Baptist University	$12,480.
Mississippi College	$11,836.
Dallas Baptist University	$11,610.
Louisiana College	$10,300.
Williams Baptist College	$8,600.

Private Texas College Tuition

Source: The Chronicle of Higher Education (October 2004)

Southern Methodist University	$25,358.
Rice University	$21,206.
Baylor University	$19,780.
Texas Christian University	$19,700.
University of Dallas	$19,162.
Letourneau University	$15,030.
Hardin-Simmons University	$13,376.
Texas Wesleyan University	$12,920.
Houston Baptist University	$12,915.
University of Mary-Hardin Baylor	$12,380.
East Texas Baptist University	$12,000.
Howard Payne University	$12,000.
Wayland Baptist University	$9,250.

California Public and Private College Tuition

Source: The Inland Empire Business Journal (February 2010)

California State Polytechnic Univ. Pomona	$3,564 / $4,272
University of California, Riverside	$2,839 / $9,709
California State University, San Bernardino	$1,350 / $1513
University of Phoenix	$475 per unit/undergrad
University of La Verne	$26,910
California State University San Marcos	$3650 / $4342
University of Redlands	$31,994
Loma Linda University	$520 per unit
California Baptist University	$23,500
Chapman University (Ontario Campus)	$345 per unit
Western University of Health Sciences	$17,500
Claremont Graduate University	$16,849
Pomona College	$35,625
Claremont McKenna College	$37,060
La Sierra University	$620 per unit

Pitzer College	$35,912
Scripps College	$37,736
Harvey Mudd College	$36,635
Brandman University (Victor Valley Campus)	$345 per unit
Western State University College of Law	$15,500
Chapman University (Coachella Valley Campus)	$345 per unit

Church of Christ Colleges and Universities Websites

Abilene Christian University
www.acu.edu

Amberton University
www.ambertonu.edu

Austin Graduate School of Theology
www.austingrad.edu

Bear Valley Bible Institute of Denver
www.bvbid.org

Cascade College
www.cascade.edu

Crowley's Ridge College
www.cre.paragould.org

David Lipscomb University
www.lipscomb.edu

Faulkner University
www.faulkner.edu

Florida College
www.flcoll.edu

Freed-Hardeman University
www.fhu.edu

Global Christian University
www.gcu.edu

Harding University
www.harding.edu

Hermitage Christian University
www.hcu.edu

Lubbock Christian University
www.lcu.edu

Magnolia Bible College
www.magnolia.edu

Nations University
www.nationsu.edu

Ohio Valley College
www.ovc.edu

Oklahoma Christian University
www.ocu.edu

Pepperdine University
www.pepperdine.edu

Rochester College
www.rc.edu

Southern Christian University
www.southernchristian.edu

Southwestern Christian College (SwCC)

Southwestern Christian College, founded and sponsored by members of Churches of Christ, is accredited as a four-year (level II), educational college (limited to **Bachelor**'s degree in Bible and Religious Education), with a two-year associate program in the liberal arts. Its purpose is to offer a holistic educational program that will motivate the student to value and achieve academic excellence within the context of commitment to moral and spiritual values. www.swcc.edu

Tennessee Bible College
www.tn-biblecollege.edu

Weston Christian College
www.w-c-c.org

York College
www.york.edu

Texas Baptist Colleges
Websites

Baptist University of the Americas	www.bua.edu
Baylor University	www.baylor.edu
Dallas Baptist University	www.dbu.edu
East Texas Baptist University	www.etbu.edu
Hardin-Simmons University	www.hsutx.edu
Houston Baptist University	www.hbu.edu
Howard Payne University	www.hputx.edu
San Marcus Baptist Academy	www.smba.edu
University of Mary Hardin-Baylor	www.umhb.edu
Wayland Baptist University	www.wbu.edu

List of historically black colleges and universities

From Wikipedia, the free encyclopedia

This list of historically black colleges and universities (HBCUs) lists institutions of higher education in the United States that were established before 1964 with the intention of serving the black community.

Alabama A&M University	Huntsville	Alabama	1875	Public		Founded as "Colored Normal School at Huntsville"
Alabama State University	Montgomery	Alabama	1867	Public		Founded as "Lincoln Normal School of Marion"
Albany State University	Albany	Georgia	1903	Public		Founded as "Albany Bible and Manual Training Institute"
Alcorn State University	Lorman	Mississippi	1871	Public		Founded as "Alcorn University" in honor of James L. Alcorn
Allen University	Columbia	South Carolina	1870	Private	African Methodist Episcopal	Founded as "Payne Institute"
American Baptist College	Nashville	Tennessee	1924	Private		Federal designation as a HBCU on March 20, 2013

U. of Arkansas at Pine Bluff	Pine Bluff	Arkansas	1873	Public		Founded as "Branch Normal College"
Arkansas Baptist College	Little Rock	Arkansas	1884	Private	Baptist	Founded as "Minister's Institute"
Barber-Scotia College	Concord	North Carolina	1867	Private	Presbyterian	Founded as two institutions, Scotia Seminary and Barber Memorial College
Benedict College	Columbia	South Carolina	1870	Private	American Baptist Churches USA	Founded as "Benedict Institute"
Bennett College	Greensboro	North Carolina	1873	Private	United Methodist Church	Founded as "Bennett Seminary"
Bethune-Cookman University	Daytona Beach	Florida	1904	Private	United Methodist Church	Founded as "Daytona Educational and Industrial Training School for Negro Girls"
Bishop State Community College	Mobile	Alabama	1927	Public		Originally a branch of Alabama State College

Bluefield State College	Bluefield	West Virginia	1895	Public		Founded as "Bluefield Colored Institute"
Bowie State University	Bowie	Maryland	1865	Public		Founded as "Baltimore Normal School"
Central State University	Wilberforce	Ohio	1887	Public	AME Church	Originally a department at Wilberforce University[5]
Cheyney University of Pennsylvania	Cheyney	Penn	1837	Public		The oldest HBCU. Founded by Quaker Richard Humphreys as "Institute for Colored Youth"
Claflin University	Orangeburg	South Carolina	1869	Private	United Methodist Church	
Clark Atlanta University	Atlanta	Georgia	1865	Private	United Methodist Church	Originally Clark Col and Atlanta U
Clinton Junior College	Rock Hill	South Carolina	1894	Private	AME Zion	Founded as "Clinton Institute"

Coahoma Community College	Coahoma County	Mississippi	1924	Public		Founded as "Coahoma County Agricultural High School"
Concordia College, Selma	Selma	Alabama	1922	Private	Lutheran Church - Missouri Synod	Known as "Alabama Lutheran Academy and Junior College" until 1981
Coppin State University	Baltimore	Maryland	1900	Public		Founded as "Colored High School"
Delaware State University	Dover	Delaware	1891	Public		Founded as "The State College for Colored Students"
Denmark Technical College	Denmark	South Carolina	1947	Public		Founded as "Denmark Area Trade School"[7]
Dillard University	New Orleans	Louisiana	1869	Private	United Church of Christ and the United Methodist Church	Founding predecessor institutions: "Straight University" and "Union Normal School"
University of the District of Columbia	Washington	District of Columbia	1851	Public		Founded as "Miner Normal School"

Edward Waters College	Jacksonville	Florida	1866	Private	AME Church	Founded as "Brown Theological Institute"
Elizabeth City State University	Elizabeth City	North Carolina	1891	Public		
Fayetteville State University	Fayetteville	North Carolina	1867	Public		Founded as "Howard School"
Fisk University	Nashville	Tennessee	1866	Private	United Church of Christ[8]	Named for Clinton Bowen Fisk
Florida A&M University	Tallahassee	Florida	1887	Public		Founded as "State Normal College for Colored Students"
Florida Memorial University	Miami Gardens	Florida	1879	Private	American Baptist Churches USA	Founded as "Florida Baptist Institute in Live Oak"
Fort Valley State University	Fort Valley	Georgia	1895	Public		Founded as "Fort Valley High and Industrial School"
Gadsden State Community College	Gadsden	Alabama	1925	Public		Founded as "Alabama School of Trades"

Grambling State University	Grambling	Louisiana	1901	Public		Founded as "Colored Industrial and Agricultural School"
Hampton University	Hampton	Virginia	1868	Private		Founded as "Hampton Normal and Agricultural Institute"
Harris-Stowe State University	St. Louis	Missouri	1857	Public		Founded as "St. Louis Normal School" for whites in 1857, with Stowe Teachers College begun in 1890 for blacks; merged in 1954
Hinds Community College at Utica	Utica	Mississippi	1903	Public		Founded as "Utica Junior College"
Howard University	Washington	District of Columbia	1867	Private		Founded as "Howard Normal and Theological School for the Education of Teachers and Preachers"
Huston-Tillotson University	Austin	Texas	1881	Private	United Methodist Church /United Church of Christ	Founded as "Tillotson Collegiate and Normal Institute"

Interdenominational Theological Center	Atlanta	Georgia	1958	Private	Interdenominational	
J. F. Drake State Technical College	Huntsville	Alabama	1961	Public		Founded as "Huntsville State Vocational Technical School"
Jackson State University	Jackson	Mississippi	1877	Public		Founded as "Natchez Seminary" by the American Baptist Home Mission Society, became public in 1942
Jarvis Christian College	Hawkins	Texas	1912	Private	The Disciples	
Johnson C. Smith University	Charlotte	North Carolina	1867	Private	Presbyterian Church (U.S.A.)	Founded as "Biddle Memorial Institute"
Kentucky State University	Frankfort	Kentucky	1886	Public		Founded as "State Normal School for Colored Persons"
Knoxville College	Knoxville (Mechanicsville)	Tennessee	1875	Private	United Presbyterian Church of North America	

Lane College	Jackson	Tennessee	1882	Private	Christian Methodist Episcopal Church	Founded as "Colored Methodist Episcopal High School"
Langston University	Langston	Oklahoma	1897	Public		Founded as "Oklahoma Colored Agricultural and Normal University"
Lawson State Community College	Bessemer	Alabama	1949	Public		
LeMoyne-Owen College	Memphis	Tennessee	1862	Private	United Church of Christ	Founded as "LeMoyne Normal and Commercial School"[11] (elementary school until 1870)
Lewis College of Business	Detroit	Michigan	1928	Private		Founded as "Lewis Business College"
Lincoln University	Chester County	Pennsylvania	1854	Public		Founded as "Ashmun Institute"
Lincoln University of Missouri	Jefferson City	Missouri	1866	Public		Founded as "Lincoln Institute"

Livingstone College	Salisbury	North Carolina	1879	Private	AME Zion	Founded as "Zion Wesley Institute"
University of Maryland Eastern Shore	Princess Anne	Maryland	1886	Public	Originally: Methodist Episcopal	Founded as "Delaware Conference Academy"
Meharry Medical College	Nashville	Tennessee	1876	Private	United Methodist Church	Founded as the Medical Department of Central Tennessee College
Miles College	Fairfield	Alabama	1905	Private	CME Church	Known until 1941 as "Miles Memorial College"; named after Bishop William H. Miles
Mississippi Valley State University	Itta Bena	Mississippi	1950	Public		Founded as "Mississippi Vocational College"
Morehouse College	Atlanta	Georgia	1867	Private	Originally, American Baptist Home Mission Society	Founded as "Augusta Institute"
Morehouse School of Medicine	Atlanta	Georgia	1975	Private		Founded originally as a part of Morehouse C

Morgan State University	Baltimore	Maryland	1867	Public	Originally: Methodist Episcopal	Founded as "Centenary Biblical Institute"
Morris Brown College	Atlanta	Georgia	1881	Private	African Methodist Episcopal	
Morris College	Sumter	South Carolina	1908	Private	Baptist Educational and Missionary Convention	
Norfolk State University	Norfolk	Virginia	1935	Public		Founded as "Norfolk Unit of Virginia State University"
North Carolina A&T State University	Greensboro	North Carolina	1891	Public		
North Carolina Central University	Durham	North Carolina	1910	Public		Founded as "National Religious Training School and Chautauqua"
Oakwood University	Huntsville	Alabama	1896	Private	Seventh-day Adventist	Founded as "Oakwood Industrial School"

Paine College	Augusta	Georgia	1882	Private	United Methodist Church and Christian Methodist Episcopal Church	Founded as "Paine Institute"
Paul Quinn College	Dallas	Texas	1872	Private	AME Church	Named for William Paul Quinn
Philander Smith College	Little Rock	Arkansas	1877	Private	United Methodist Church	Founded as "Walden Seminary"
Prairie View A&M University	Prairie View	Texas	1876	Public		Founded as "Alta Vista Agriculture & Mechanical College for Colored Youth"[15]
Rust College	Holly Springs	Mississippi	1866	Private	United Methodist Church	Known as "Shaw University" until 1882
Savannah State University	Savannah	Georgia	1890	Public		Founded as "Georgia State Industrial College for Colored Youth"
Selma University	Selma	Alabama	1878	Private	Alabama State Missionary Baptist Convention	Founded as "Alabama Baptist Normal and Theological School"

Shaw University	Raleigh	North Carolina	1865	Private	National Baptist Convention, USA, Inc.	
Shorter College	Little Rock	Arkansas	1886	Private	African Methodist Episcopal	Unaccredited two-year college; founded as "Bethel University"
Shelton State Community College	Tuscaloosa	Alabama	1952	Public		Founded as "J.P. Shelton Trade School"
South Carolina State University	Orangeburg	South Carolina	1896	Public		Founded as "Colored, Normal, Industrial, Agricultural, and Mechanical College of South Carolina"
Southern University at New Orleans	New Orleans	Louisiana	1959	Public		Founded as a branch unit of Southern University in Baton Rouge
Southern University at Shreveport	Shreveport	Louisiana	1967	Public		Part of the Southern University System
Southern University and A&M College	Baton Rouge	Louisiana	1881	Public		Conceptualized by P. B. S. Pinchback, T. T. Allain, and Henry Demas

Southwestern Christian College	Terrell	Texas	1948	Private	Church of Christ	Founded as "Southern Bible Institute"
Spelman College	Atlanta	Georgia	1881	Private	Originally,American Baptist Home Mission Society	Founded as "Atlanta Baptist Female Seminary"
St. Augustine's University	Raleigh	North Carolina	1867	Private	Episcopal Church (United States)	
St. Philip's College	San Antonio	Texas	1898	Public	Episcopal Church	Founded as "St. Philip's Sewing Class for Girls"
Stillman College	Tuscaloosa	Alabama	1876	Private		Founded as Tuscaloosa Institute, the College was a concept of Reverend Dr. Charles Allen Stillman, pastor of First Presbyterian Church of Tuscaloosa
Talladega College	Talladega County	Alabama	1867	Private	United Church of Christ	Known as "Swayne School" until 1869
Tennessee State University	Nashville	Tennessee	1912	Public		Founded as "Ag and Industrial State Normal School"

Texas College	Tyler	Texas	1894	Private	Christian Methodist Episcopal	
Texas Southern University	Houston	Texas	1927	Public		Founded as "Texas State University for Negroes"
Tougaloo College	Hinds County	Mississippi	1869	Private	American Missionary Association	Founded as "Tougaloo University"
Trenholm State Technical College	Montgomery	Alabama	1947	Public		Founded as "John M. Patterson Technical School"
Tuskegee University	Tuskegee	Alabama	1881	Private		Founded as Tuskegee Institute, now a National Historic Site
University of the Virgin Islands	St. Croix & St. Thomas	United States Virgin Islands	1962	Public		Founded as "College of the Virgin Islands"
Virginia State University	Petersburg	Virginia	1882	Public		Founded as "Virginia Normal and Collegiate Institute at Petersburg"

Virginia Union University	Richmond	Virginia	1864	Private	American Baptist Churches USA	Founded as "Wayland Seminary," and merged with Richmond Institute (1865) in 1889
Virginia University of Lynchburg	Lynchburg	Virginia	1886	Private	Baptist	Founded as "Lynchburg Baptist Seminary"
Voorhees College	Denmark	South Carolina	1897	Private	Episcopal Church	Founded as "Denmark Industrial School"
West Virginia State University	Kanawha County	West Virginia	1891	Public		Founded as "West VA Colored Institute"
Wilberforce University	Wilberforce	Ohio	1856	Private	AME Church	Named for William Wilberforce
Wiley College	Marshall	Texas	1873	Private	United Methodist Church	Named for Isaac William Wiley
Winston-Salem State University	Winston-Salem	North Carolina	1892	Public		Founded as "Slater Industrial and State Normal School"

Henry O. Adkins

Xavier University of Louisiana	New Orleans	Louisiana	1915	Private	Roman Catholic	Founding predecessor institutions: "St. Katharine Drexel" and the "Sisters of the Blessed Sacrament"

NOTES _____

_____

_____

_____

_____

_____

_____

_____

_____

This workbook is designed to benefit anyone looking for a successful College education and experience. Common Sense will get you into a good school. It will also get you through your College experience and take you on to a successful career.

Henry O. Adkins has been married to Sue L. Adkins for 47 years. They met their freshman year in College. They have three children, all college graduates with jobs. "The number one thing in my life", he states, "is watching my children grow and develop into successful college educated citizens." Henry O is a graduate of Dallas Baptist University (BS) and the University of North Texas (MPA). The love of his life (wife Sue) is a graduate of Texas Woman's University (BS) and Southern Methodist University (MPA). She is an author and playwright. His daughter is an attorney, one son is a supervisor for Delta Airlines and one son is a writer. Henry O, Sue and their children all used Common Sense to successfully complete college and graduate school.

This workbook is designed to help you achieve the best for a successful College education, and experience. Common sense will get you into a good school. It will also get you ahead in your College experience and take you on to a successful career.

www.cheudi.com

www.ingramcontent.com/pod-product-compliance
Lightning Source LLC
Chambersburg PA
CBHW081150090426
42736CB00017B/3256